Enhancing Investment Promotion in Tajikistan

OECD
BETTER POLICIES FOR BETTER LIVES

Please cite this publication as:
OECD (2022), *Enhancing Investment Promotion in Tajikistan*, OECD Publishing, Paris, https://doi.org/10.1787/1e3a7c4f-en.

ISBN 978-92-64-64892-0 (print)
ISBN 978-92-64-53737-8 (pdf)
ISBN 978-92-64-50990-0 (HTML)
ISBN 978-92-64-39688-3 (epub)

Photo credits: Cover © AlisaRut/Shutterstock.com.

Corrigenda to publications may be found on line at: www.oecd.org/about/publishing/corrigenda.htm.

Foreword

Tajikistan (throughout the report, Tajikistan is used to indicate the Republic of Tajikistan) is working to improve the country's investment environment and facilitate the inflow of FDI. At the same time, it is increasing its investment-promotion efforts, recognising that improvements in the investment climate and targeted investment promotion practices must go hand in hand to attract investors to Tajikistan.

An OECD public-private Working Group (WG) was created in early 2021 to help design targeted policies to feed into Tajikistan's investment promotion practices. The WG met virtually three times in 2021. It was chaired by the First Deputy Chair of the State Committee of Investment and State Property Management (SCISPM), currently Mr Khurshed Mirzo. The WG brought together stakeholders from different ministries, the State Committee for Investment and State Property Management (SCISPM), investors, business associations, and NGOs active in the field, as well as representatives of the development community.

This peer review note reflects the work of the WG as well as the contribution of international experts from Kazakhstan, France and Georgia. The final recommendations outlined in the note were peer reviewed during the OECD Eurasia Competitiveness Roundtable end 2021 in a virtual manner as part of a series of OECD Eurasia webinars. This exercise involved both international experts and representatives from OECD member countries and other Central Asian countries

Acknowledgements

This note summarises work carried out by the OECD Eurasia Competitiveness Programme in consultation with the Tajik government, in close collaboration with the development community in Tajikistan, and with the participation of the private sector and business associations. The project was funded principally by the European Union and serves as the Policy Component of the Central Asia Invest Programme. The OECD would like to thank the representatives of ministries, the private sector, business associations, non-governmental organisations, and other stakeholders for their willingness to share valuable insights that contributed to the development of this note. The work was overseen on the Tajik side by His Excellency Mr Davlatali Said, the First Deputy Prime Minister of Tajikistan.

The OECD would like to extend its gratitude to the following representatives of State Committee for Investment and State Property Management and Tajinvest: Mr Khurshed Mirzo, Current First Deputy Chairman; and Mr Merali Bodurshozoda, Head of the Single Window Unit on Investor Assistance. From Tajinvest the OECD would like to thank Mr Javokhirlai Muzaffari, Executive Director; and Mr Hans-Joachim Siegert, Expert in Tajinvest. The OECD would also like to recognise the contributions made by: Mr Ayubjon Maruf Solehzoda, First Deputy Chairman of the Tax Committee and Mr Umejon Khairiddinov, Deputy Head of the International Co-operation Department of the Tax Committee, Mr. Yusuf Majidi, Deputy Minister of Finance and Mr. Numon Abdughafforzoda, Head of the Secretariat of the Consultative Council on the Improvement of the Investment Climate.

Representatives of the private sector and business associations provided useful inputs during virtual discussions, and we are particularly grateful to: Ms Elena Son, Executive Director, of the US-Tajikistan Business Council; Mr Jamshed Jumakhonzoda of the Chamber of Commerce and Industry; and Mr Jean-Jacques Kudela, **Team Leader,** Digital transition expert, **Digital Capabilities Strategic Analysis of Tajikistan**[1]**.** Similarly, the OECD thanks the interviewees from the private sector who dedicated their time to this report.

We also thank the international experts that provided valuable contributions to the report: Mr Tornike Zirakishvili, Enterprise Georgia; Mr Philippe Yvergniaux, Business France; and Ms Diana Ablyakimova, Kazakh Invest. The OECD Secretariat also received invaluable local support from Ms Veronika Grushevskaya in Tajikistan.

A number of representatives of the development community and academia provided further support to the work: Jan Peter Olters, former Country Director of the World Bank in Tajikistan; Nuraddin Murshudlu and Filippo Crivellaro, both Economic Officers at the OSCE; Muhammadi Boboev, Senior Economics Officer, at the Asian Development Bank (ADB); Anvar Ibragimov and Madina Nurmatova, both Operations Officers at the IFC, and lastly, both Anel Pirmakhanova and Nodira Mansurova, at the EBRD.

Finally, this report would not have been possible without the continued financial and diplomatic support of the European Union. Thanks are due to Mr Pierre Amilhat, Director, Directorate-General for International Co-operation and Development (DG DEVCO), European Commission (EC); Ms Raffaela Iodice, Head of Unit DEVCO Middle East, Central Asia, South Asia, DG DEVCO, F1 Unit, EC; Mr Daniel Weiss, Development Co-ordinator, Central Asia, DG DEVCO, EC; Mr Thomas Boyer, Programme Manager, DG

DEVCO; Mr Johannes Stenbaek Madsen, Head of Co-operation Section, EU Delegation to Kazakhstan; Ms Silvia Pietropaolo, Programme Manager, EU Delegation to Kazakhstan; Mr Stefano Ellero, former Head of Co-operation of the EU Delegation to Tajikistan, Mr Marc Buchmann, current Head of Co-operation of the EU Delegation to Tajikistan, and Mr Francesco Straniero, Attaché at the EU Delegation to Tajikistan.

This report was prepared under the guidance of Mr Andreas Schaal, Director, OECD Global Relations and Co-operation; and Mr William Tompson, Head of the OECD Eurasia Division. The work was co-ordinated by Mr Grégory Lecomte, Head of the Central Asia Unit, OECD Eurasia Division. The main authors of this report are Ms Talisa zur Hausen and Ms Katrina Keegan, both Policy Analysts in the OECD Eurasia Division, with contributions from Mr Alexis Patin and Mr César Bernard, both Junior Policy Analysts in the OECD Eurasia Division. The report was reviewed by, and benefited from valuable input from, Mr Alexander Böhmer, Head of the South East Asia Division, Ms Peline Atamer, Deputy Head of Unit for Ukraine, and Mr Francesco Alfonso, Deputy Head of Unit for Eastern Europe and the South Caucasus, OECD Eurasia Division, and Ms Amélie Schurich, Economist and Policy Analyst, OECD Eurasia Division. Final editorial and visual support was provided by Ms Elisa Larrakoetxea and Ms Mariana Tanova, OECD Eurasia Division.

Table of contents

FIGURES

BOXES

Acronyms and Abbreviations

ABA	Austrian Business Agency
ADB	Asian Development Bank
BCG	Boston Consulting Group
B2B	Business-to-business
BITs	Bilateral investment treaties
CCI	Chamber of Commerce and Industry
CRM	Customer relationship management
EBRD	European Bank for Reconstruction and Development
FEZ	Free economic zone
FDI	Foreign Direct Investment
GDP	Gross domestic product
GIZ	Deutsche Gesellschaft für Internationale Zusammenarbeit
IDA	Industrial Development Authority (Ireland)
IMF	International Monetary Fund
IPA	Investment Promotion Agency
KOTRA	Korea Trade-Investment Promotion Agency
LAC	Latin America and the Caribbean
LIAA	Latvia Investment and Development Agency
LOI	Law on Investments
NAS	National development strategy
NFIA	Netherlands Foreign Investment Agency
OECD	Organization for Economic Co-operation and Development
OSCE	Organization for Security and Co-Operation in Europe
PPD	Public-private dialog
SARIO	Slovak Investment and Trade Development Agency
SCISPM	State Committee on Investment and State Property
SEO	Search engine optimization
SME	Small and medium sized enterprises
SOE	State-owned enterprise
UNCTAD	United Nations Conference on Trade and Development
UNESCAP	United Nations Economic and Social Commission for Asia and the Pacific
USD	US dollar (currency)
VAT	Value Added Tax
WAIPA	World Association of Investment Promotion Agencies
WG	Working Group
WTO	World Trade Organization

Key indicators for Tajikistan

Population, 2020	9.475 million (IMF)
Surface area, 2020	141,400 km2 (World Bank)
GDP (current prices), 2020	USD 8 billion[1] (Ministry of Finance)
GDP per capita (current prices), 2020	USD 849[2] (Ministry of Economic Development and Trade)
Real GDP growth (y-o-y change), 2020	4.5% (IMF)
Share of primary sector value added in GDP, 2020	23.8% (World Bank)
Share of secondary sector value added in GDP, 2020	32.8% (World Bank)
Share of tertiary sector value added in GDP, 2020	35.3% (World Bank)
Inflation (average consumer prices, y-o-y change), 2020	9.4% (TAJSTAT)
Official currency conversion rate (somoni / USD), 2020	9.53 (TAJSTAT)
PPP currency conversion rate (somoni / USD), 2020	2.3 (IMF)
Exports of goods and services (% of GDP), 2020	17.0% (World Bank)
Imports of goods and services (% of GDP), 2020	38.2% (World Bank)
Current account balance (% of GDP), 2019	-2.283% (IMF)
FDI stock, 2020	USD 3.128 billion (UNCTAD)
FDI stock (% of GDP), 2020	38.2% (UNCTAD)
FDI net inflows, 2019	USD 213 million (World Bank)
FDI, net inflows (% of GDP), 2019	2.5% (World Bank)
Government expenditure (% of GDP), 2020	29.7% (IMF)
Government revenues (% of GDP), 2020	25.3% (IMF)
General government net lending/ borrowing (% of GDP), 2019	-2.1% (IMF)
Government debt (% of GDP), 2020	44.1%[3] (IMF)
Labour force participation rate (% of total population ages 15+), 2020	41.5% (World Bank)
Unemployment (% of total labour force, ILO estimate), 2020	7.2%[4](Ministry of Finance)
Personal remittances received (% of GDP), 2020	26.7%
Poverty rate (national poverty line), 2020	26.3% (World Bank)
Lending interest rate, 2020	23.6% (World Bank)
Total number of SMEs (units), 2019	30 000 (EBRD)
Total number of SOEs (units), 2019	920 (EBRD)
Total number of joint-stock companies (units), 2019	140 (EBRD)
Net official development assistance (% of GNI), 2020	3.8% (World Bank)

1. 8.19 billion according to the IMF
2. 851.11 according to the IMF
3. 7.3% according to the Ministry of Finance of Tajikistan
4. 7.5% according to the World Bank

Executive Summary

Tajikistan has identified FDI as a critical component of its national development strategy, but the country faces challenges in attracting sufficient investment to non-extractive sectors. FDI can help Tajikistan achieve many of its economic goals, including job creation, diversification and private-sector development. Therefore, FDI attraction can be an important component of Tajikistan's recovery and structural transformation. Yet despite statutory openness to investment in most sectors, Tajikistan has not yet fully realised its potential as an investment destination, and foreign investment is concentrated in extractive industries. It needs to attract more and more diverse FDI inflows in terms of both sources and destination sectors.

Investment promotion and facilitation actions carried out by a dedicated investment promotion agency (IPA) can help attract FDI when underpinned by other measures to improve the investment framework. As the pandemic is expected to increase competition for FDI and reduce investors' appetite for risk globally, the role of IPAs is gaining importance around the world. Stronger investment promotion may be especially critical for Tajikistan, as many international investors still know relatively little about it, and they must therefore devote significant resources to gathering information about opportunities and challenges there. An effective IPA can reduce these costs through proactive outreach to potential investors. It can also help reduce the cost of doing business by helping investors navigate the country's complex and often unpredictable legal environment.

This note provides analysis and recommendations to strengthen investment promotion in Tajikistan and support the attraction of more FDI, focusing on (1) promotional activities (2) the institutional framework for investment promotion, and (3) facilitation and policy advocacy functions.

First, activities. At present, investors can find it difficult to locate information about investment opportunities in Tajikistan. The country would benefit from clearer branding as an investment destination, through clear and consistent messaging by leveraging digital platforms. It would also be helpful to identify a limited number of sectors to target for investment – an important endeavour given limited resources. Tajikistan's IPAs might also reduce their reliance on time-intensive but less effective methods, like generalised events. Some simple and potentially effective solutions, such as a well-designed website and database to track prospective investors, could enable the authorities to identify and contact them proactively.

Second, institutions. Currently, Tajikistan has one main government institution mandated with investment promotion. The State Committee on Investment and State Property Management is the authorised body to promote and develop investment. The State Unitary Enterprise "Tajinvest", which operates under the Committee's umbrella, fulfils a number of key functions. In addition, other line ministries have departments involved in investment promotion and facilitation in their relevant sectors. Some investors report finding it hard to understand the distinctions between their mandates and activities, which can contribute to confusion and inefficiency. Streamlining and clarifying for investors and other external actors the roles of these institutions would help them realise their investment-promotion mandates. Tajikistan at this point also lacks the development of an overarching investment strategy with specific goals and methods for investment promotion. Such a strategy is needed to guide, co-ordinate and focus the work of all these actors.

Third, policy advocacy and facilitation. Prospective and current investors report that they can face significant procedural and legal hurdles in their investment journey. While Tajikistan's IPA devotes significant resources to providing assistance with these issues, investors note that this support can be limited. The State Committee is actively engaged in generalised aftercare and they emphasise their readiness to help resolve individual problems, but investors report being uncertain about when and how to rely on them in respect of specific disputes (taxation, inspections, permits, etc.). Maintaining good relationships with existing investors by offering logistical facilitation and aftercare services could help change this. This includes liaising with investors to advocate on their behalf in order to assess and smoothen bottlenecks in the investment climate.

It is critical that Tajikistan continues to advance reforms to improve the overall investment environment in tandem with steps to strengthen investment promotion. In recent years, the authorities have simplified regulation in many spheres, introduced measures to reduce administrative burdens on businesses and substantially overhauled the tax code. These are welcome steps and it is critical that they continue even as the country strengthens its promotion institutions and strategies.

Introduction

The main drivers of growth in Tajikistan

Since the turn of the century, GDP growth has officially averaged 7.7% per annum (Figure 1), albeit slowing slightly over the last decade as the economy rebounded from the Soviet era. Up until September 2021, Tajikistan's real GDP grew at an annual rate of 8.9%, as the country bounced back from the COVID-19 shock of 2020 (World Bank, 2021[1]) (OECD, 2021[2]). GDP measured in constant 2010 USD rose from 2.6 billion in 2000 to 10.9 billion in 2021. As a result, from 2000 to 2019, the share of the population below the national poverty line fell from 83% to 26.3% (World Bank, 2019[3]; World Bank, 2021[4]). There is still considerable scope for catch-up growth, though; per capita GDP in 2020 was estimated at USD 3858 in purchasing power parity terms (2017 constant international dollars) (World Bank, 2020).

Figure 1. GDP growth (1988-2020) in Tajikistan and the production structure of GDP in 2019

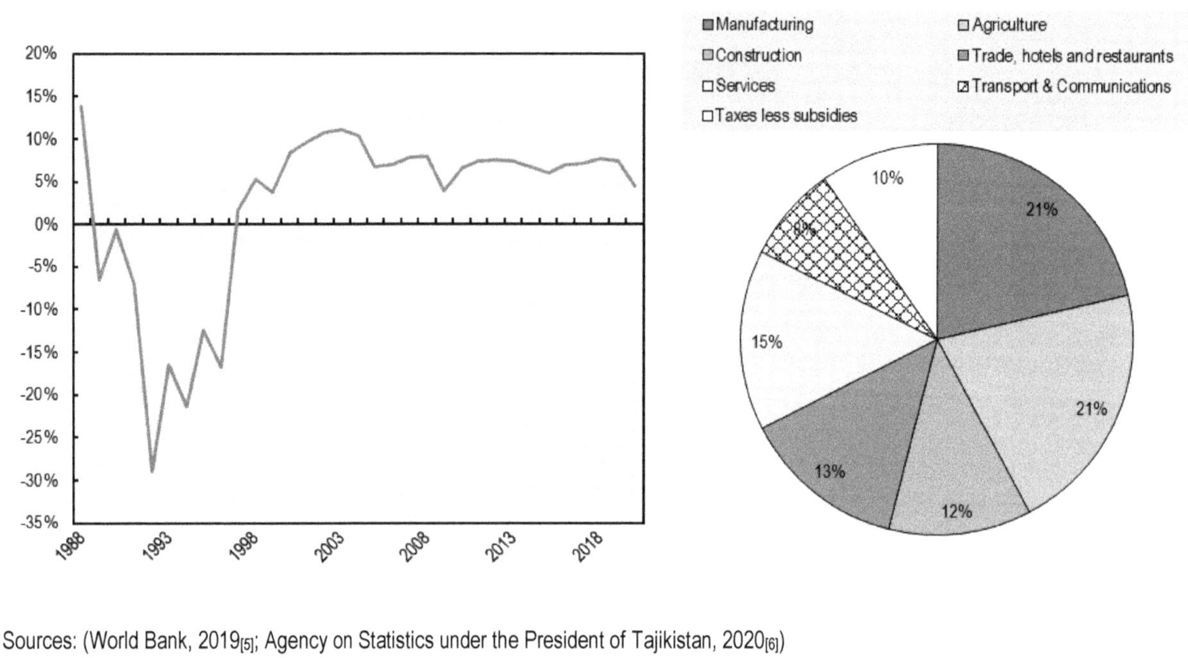

Sources: (World Bank, 2019[5]; Agency on Statistics under the President of Tajikistan, 2020[6])

Growth has been driven to a substantial extent by the government's policy of channelling high levels of public investment into large-scale infrastructure projects. However, it could be difficult to sustain this approach over the long-term, as general government gross debt has risen significantly since the mid-2010s from 28% of GDP in 2014 to an estimated 44% in 2019, narrowing the government's fiscal space (IMF, 2021[7]). This highlights the need to mobilise greater private investment – which is both a challenge and a huge opportunity for Tajikistan.

Remittances from labour migrants working abroad constitute a major source of income for the country, equivalent to 26.7% of GDP in 2020 (Agency on Statistics under the President of Tajikistan, 2020[6]). While some remittances are saved or invested, 57% are used for immediate consumption. Moreover, they have fluctuated considerably over time, in response to developments abroad (Figure 2). Increasing FDI, particularly into sectors that would generate more and more productive jobs, could substantially reduce the country's vulnerability to external shocks linked to changes in export prices or remittance flows.

Figure 2. Oil price movements and migrant remittances received by Tajikistan (2002-2020)

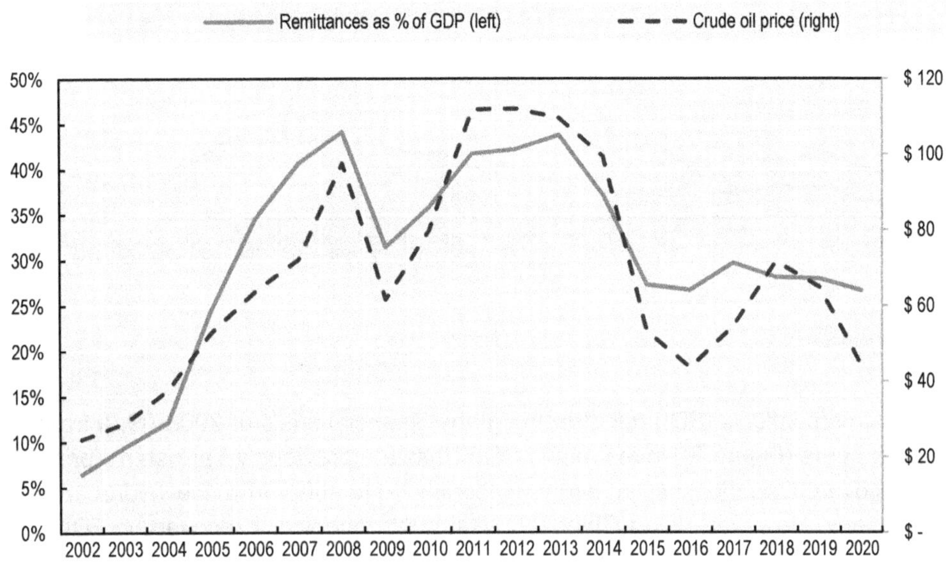

Sources: (World Bank, 2021[8]; OECD, 2021[9])

The COVID-19 pandemic slowed growth to 4.5% in Tajikistan in 2020. Restrictions on labour mobility and economic activity resulted in lower remittances, weaker consumer demand, and a reduction in investment (OECD, 2020[10]; World Bank, 2020[11]). Despite the crisis, the Statistical Agency under President of the Republic of Tajikistan reported real GDP growth of 8.9% by September 2021 (ADB, 2021[12]).

Foreign direct investment trends in Tajikistan

Annual FDI inflows during 1999-2019 averaged 4.3% of GDP (Figure 3), below the average for the OECD Eurasia region of 6.3% but close to the regional average of 5.1% if one excludes the main oil and gas exporters[2]. This has led to an accumulated FDI stock of 38.65% of GDP in Tajikistan as of 2020, compared to an average of 55.84% in Central Asia (UNCTAD, 2020[13]). In dollar terms, Tajikistan's inward FDI stock stood at USD 3.1 billion before the pandemic (UNCTAD, 2020[13]). At the same time, according to the SCISPM, the country attracted 150 bn somoni (USD 14 bn) in foreign investment (both FDI and other foreign investment) since 2001. However, FDI inflows fell by 53% in 2020[3] (greater than the estimated global drop of 42%). Global flows rebounded, albeit unevenly, in 2021, but the outlook for Tajikistan and the world remains clouded by uncertainties about the pandemic and recovery prospects (UNCTAD, 2021[14]). However, the pandemic may also open some opportunities for FDI as firms seek greater resilience through geographic diversification, including cost-cutting, nearshoring and offshoring, which will primarily affect developing countries like Tajikistan (OECD, 2020[15]).

Figure 3. Inward FDI as a % of GDP, 3-year moving average

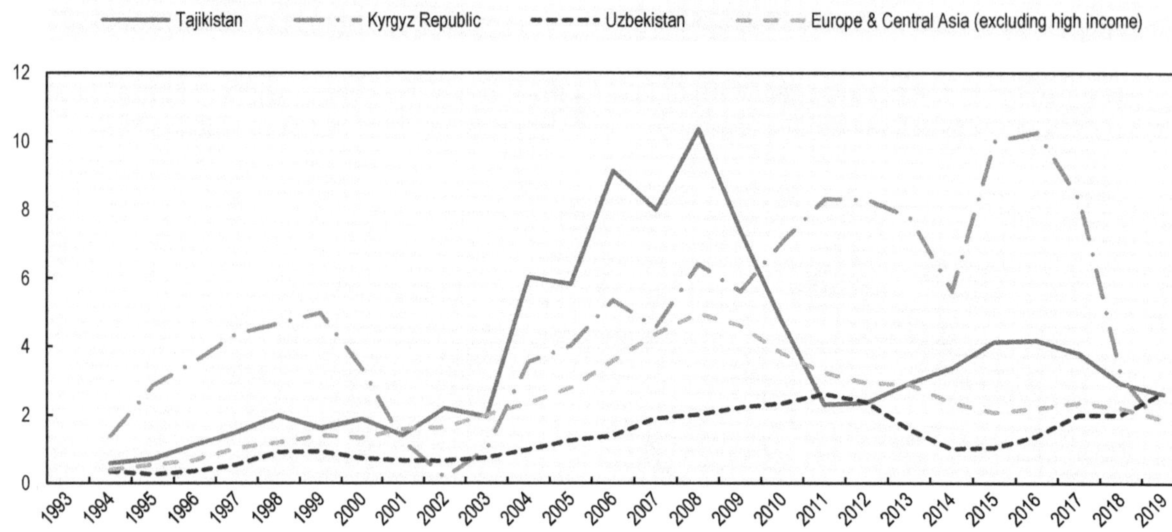

Source: (World Bank, 2021[16])

Foreign direct investment inflows (FDI) fell after the global financial crisis of 2008-09, a trend common to Tajikistan's regional peers (Figure 3). Investments from Russia – previously Tajikistan's primary source of FDI – never fully recovered, as the Russian economy continued to suffer from low hydrocarbon prices and then Western sanctions. However, rising Chinese investments enabled a recovery in FDI inflows during the 2010s, and these now constitute the bulk of inward flows (Figure 4). Inflows remain relatively concentrated in terms of sectors.

Investment in Tajikistan has been overwhelmingly driven by public funds (in 2020, only 25% of investment came from private sources of finance) and thus are concentrated in the government's priority sectors, particularly aluminium, cotton, and energy (Santander Trade, 2021[17]). In 2018, the mining sector received 61% of total FDI (USD 221m) (World Bank, 2020[11]). According to data provided by the SCISPM, this proportion remained nearly unchanged (64%) during the pandemic, although in absolute terms the volume fell in line with the overall drop in FDI during the first stages of the COVID-19 crisis. As FDI inflows continue to be concentrated in the extractive sector, their volume is linked more closely to global demand and pricing for extractive goods than to the investment climate environment per se (EBRD, 2020[18]).

Figure 4. Incoming FDI to Tajikistan by country (2009-2020) and sector (in absolute USD figures)

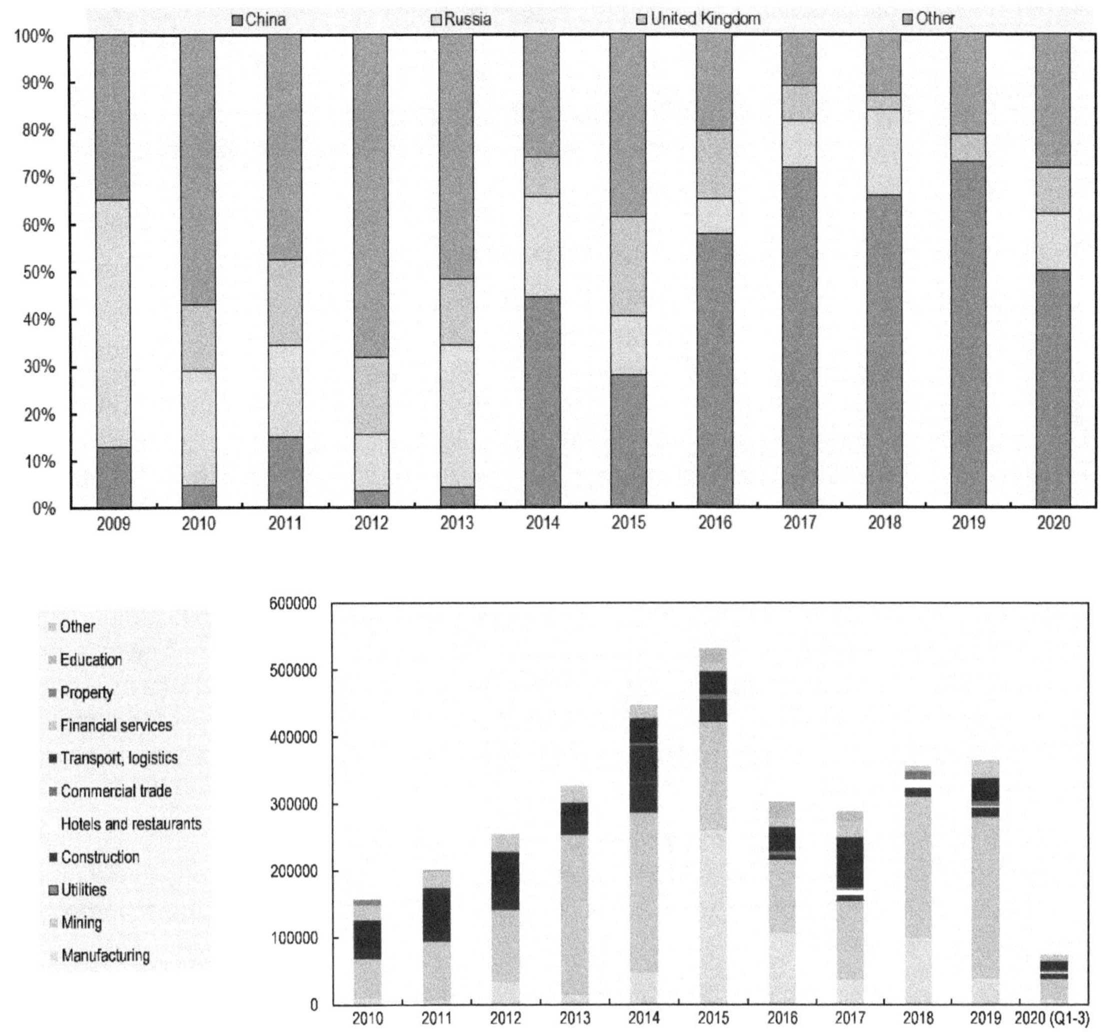

Source: Compiled data from annual U.S. Investment Climate Reports for Tajikistan; (National Bank of Tajikistan, 2020[19])

Tajikistan would benefit from more diversified FDI inflows

Given fewer alternative domestic private or public sources of capital and the need to recover from the pandemic, Tajikistan needs more diversified FDI (Embassy of Switzerland in Tajikistan, 2020[19]; OECD, 2020[10]; OECD, 2021[2]). There are many good reasons for the country to want to diversify FDI flows and, in particular, attract FDI to manufacturing and other non-resource tradables. This would not only reduce the economy's vulnerability to commodity-price fluctuations, but also generate more – and more productive – formal-sector jobs. Resource extraction, which is capital- rather than labour-intensive, generates relatively little employment. More diversified FDI flows will also indirectly create employment opportunities and promote entrepreneurship and SME development through supplier linkages. These investments open new markets to domestic companies through their integration in the international production chains of MNEs and are accompanied by transfers of skills and technology.

This ambition has important implications for policy. Many economies have done well in attracting FDI to the extractive sector but not elsewhere. The conventional typology of FDI (resource- seeking, market-seeking and efficiency-seeking) is instructive here. Resource-seeking FDI in the extraction sector in some ways resembles public procurement, since the subsoil is state property. The government knows what it wants and so does the investor, so the government has to choose among competing investors – in effect, competing service-providers – to extract the primary resource. The chosen investor is supposed to deliver what it and the government agree *ex ante*. Often, there is little trust, because the government sees the investor as keen to exploit a resource that belongs to the state, but the investor is needed for his capital, expertise, etc. Even when trust is low, agreement can often be reached because the potential paybacks are high and the major variables affecting the economics of the project are well understood. Tajikistan is no exception to the rule. The extractive sector requires additional investment in branches in which the country should be a leading regional player, such as aluminium and hydropower, to increase their competitiveness and tap a larger share of unexploited potential.

Beyond extractive materials, which are dependent on global commodity prices, foreign investments in new promising sectors could help diversify economic activity in Tajikistan. They require a rather different approach to foreign investment. Market- and efficiency- seeking investments in manufacturing and other non-extractive sectors are more closely linked to institutional quality and investment policy settings. There is much less known *ex ante* about the potential investment's viability and profitability. This means investors generate new opportunities rather than compete for pre-existing ones, and in response, the government has to be far less risk-averse and far readier to ease restrictions. This entails willingness to trust, rather than control, foreign investors. The conviction that the investor is there to exploit the locals' resources, and must therefore be subject to close scrutiny every step of the way, will impede potentially productive investment. Moreover, when foreign investors are smaller, they are more likely to rely on general framework conditions for business and investment rather than on deal- or project-specific mechanisms like tailored concessions or production-sharing agreements. They are also less likely to have the internal resources to make up for deficits in public goods provision (security, infrastructure, etc.). This implies that these other forms of FDI will depend on the overall business environment far more than investment in large-scale resource extraction.

In Tajikistan, agricultural processing, the petrochemical industry and tourism are deemed promising sectors that for efficiency-seeking investments. To ensure this, the government needs to define clearly which specific sectors both have an attractive value proposition and meet Tajikistan's development goals, then target investors accordingly.

For both types of investments, dynamic demographics and high labour supply are key. The population has been growing steadily at a rate of 2.4% over the last five years. However, the labour participation rate amounted to 41.5% in 2020, way below the OECD average (61.1%, 2020) and peer countries like Kyrgyzstan (58.81%, 2018) or Kazakhstan (69%, 2020). Therefore, well-designed employment policies are needed to increase labour-force participation and create the skills needed in sectors that could thrive with new foreign investment. Integration in the region will also be critical, given that Tajikistan remains, in global terms, a small market: FDI attraction will be more likely to succeed where conditions for export are more promising.

Tajikistan's natural resources, especially gold, silver and antimony, are currently the main sources of export earnings. However, some sectors' profitability could be improved with additional investments, making access to international finance crucial. Apart from traditional products such as aluminium or hydroelectricity, which are very dependent on global commodity prices, foreign investments in new promising sectors could help diversify the economic activity (agricultural processing, petrochemicals and tourism). To ensure that sectors with potential are able to attract the FDI they require, the government needs to understand and communicate the value propositions of these sectors and then target investors accordingly.

Investment promotion must be part of efforts to diversify production, employment and exports

As a relatively small economy in the heart of Central Asia, Tajikistan is a relatively little-known to potential investors in many regions of the world; many global investors may not be aware of its potential or have experience doing business there. This means that significant research on their end is necessary to learn about opportunities and navigate the logistics of investing. As some investors come to the country, others can benefit from the information generated by the first movers, which makes it even less appealing for investors to be pioneers (they would be generating positive spill-overs to the benefit of potential competitors). Nor do investors consider the positive externalities for domestic businesses. These considerations provide a justification for public intervention (OECD, 2018[20]; OECD & Inter-American Development Bank, 2019[21]).

Centralised investment promotion agencies can be instrumental in resolving such market failures by both *promoting* and *facilitating* investment (OECD, 2019[22]; OECD, 2015[23]). To *promote* investment, IPAs usually conduct image-building and outreach activities, including marketing through their websites and promotional materials and public relations events, such as road shows, forums, and missions abroad. These can brand the host country as a profitable investment destination. IPAs also engage in specific outreach to prospective investors. To *facilitate* investment, IPAs provide administrative assistance to prospective and existing investors, with support for the latter serving to encourage reinvestment and contribute to the country's favourable reputation. These close interactions with investors allow IPAs to grasp their challenges and channel them to policymakers through their policy advocacy function, thereby improving the overall investment climate.

This report, drawing on OECD expertise in IPAs, will help the Tajik government realise its goals of increased and diversified FDI and continuing to improve the investment climate

The government of Tajikistan has defined the attraction of foreign investment and the creation of a favourable business climate that enables it as national policy priorities in its 2030 *National Development Strategy* (NDS) and the *Medium-term Development Strategy* for 2021-25. The NDS sets a target of attracting more than USD 55 bn in FDI by 2030.

To achieve this very ambitious goal, the government has enacted a number of legal and regulatory reforms to improve the investment climate (OECD, 2021[2]). These reforms include the simplification of administrative requirements, encompassing the reduction of licenses and permits from 605 to 64 and the increased ease of obtaining them. Tajikistan introduced a risk-based mechanism to select candidates for inspection in order to improve regulatory effectiveness while reducing the burden on firms; created a co-ordination council, and instituted a moratorium on business inspections, which has been in place since January 2019. An online portal tajtrade.tj has detailed import and export information on selected goods, including required documents. Tajikistan has also made significant improvements in facilitating access to credit. Many other reforms are planned or ongoing in areas such as justice, procurement, and taxation. *De jure*, Tajikistan is very open to investment (OECD, 2021[2]). The OECD FDI Restrictiveness Index, which measures statutory limitations to FDI, shows the country close to the average for non-OECD economies in most sectors and in line with regional peers. Indeed, Tajikistan has no laws discriminating against foreign investors by conditioning, limiting or prohibiting overseas investment in any economic sectors (OECD, 2021[2]).

Figure 5. OECD 2019 FDI Regulatory Restrictiveness Index: sectoral restrictions in Tajikistan

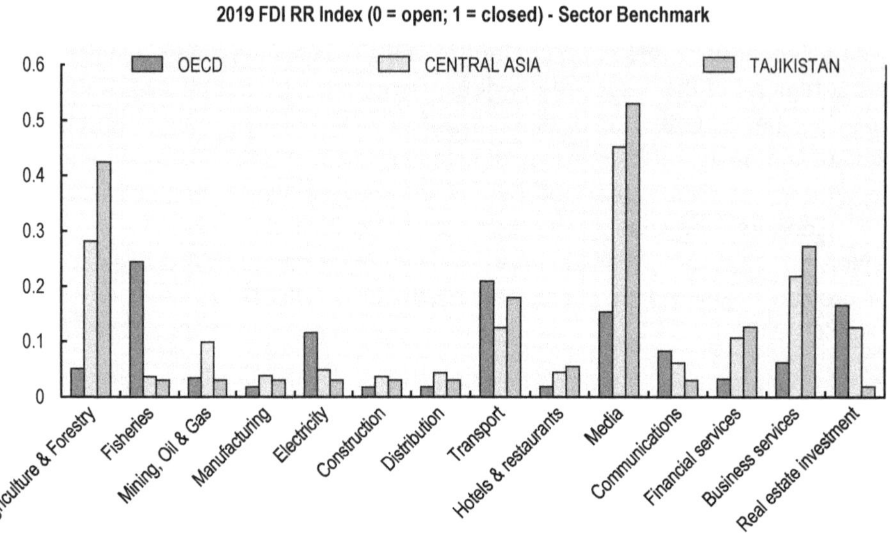

Note: Open=0, closed=1
Source:OECD FDI Regulatory Restrictiveness Index

For now, Tajikistan ranks 104th on the World Economic Forum's Global Competitiveness Index (Schwab, 2019[24]). It is critical that Tajikistan's IPA takes advantage of this moment to inform investors about new opportunities and assist them in overcoming the remaining barriers. This paper thus argues that an updated and realistic strategy, including methods of targeting and facilitating investment, can help Tajikistan attract investors and convince them to continue investing even in the midst of a protracted crisis. Such efforts must, however, be undertaken in the context of concrete steps to improve the legal environment for business, as discussed in the OECD report *Improving the Legal Environment for Business in Central Asia* (2021[2]). Investment promotion can only succeed when the investment environment really is attractive to investors. It cannot offset defects in that environment.

Drawing on OECD expertise with IPAs in OECD and partner countries, this report makes the following recommendations:

I. Raise investor awareness of Tajikistan's strengths, branding it as an attractive investment destination through clear and consistent messaging and leveraging digital platforms. Given pressure on public finances and the need for economic diversification, Tajikistan's IPAs have an incentive to select priority sectors for promotion to allocate strained resources. Systematising information-sharing among them about investors using a database and targeted outreach will help attract high-quality investments.

II. Clarify the institutional architecture of investment promotion to avoid duplication and overlap and put in place a strategy that is up to date with respect to Tajikistan's evolving needs and challenges.

III. Retain investors already in Tajikistan by offering logistical facilitation and aftercare services, which can encourage re-investment. This mainly includes closely liaising with investors to identify bottlenecks in the investment climate to provide evidence-based policy recommendations to the government.

In addition to the specific recommendations presented in this report, several cross-cutting themes apply to all topics (see Way Forward): ensuring a whole-of-government approach to adopting the recommendations, maximising the ability of limited IPA staff to achieve the recommendations, and making use of the international knowledge community to help implement these recommendations and continue adopting best practices in the future.

Recommendation 1. Ensure IPAs use consistent messaging and proper tools for promotional activities

Challenge: Tajikistan does not approach investors with clear messages and effective digital tools

Tajikistan's investment promotion efforts suffer from the absence of a clear value proposition and narrow definition of priority sectors

Tajikistan could improve its efforts in creating a recognisable image for most potential foreign investors. Generating such an image requires clear and consistent messaging about what it can offer investors, that is, a compelling value proposition. The three major selling points to investors identified by the SCISPM in the 2021 OECD questionnaire – macroeconomic and political stability, a young and well-educated workforce, and a harmonised regulatory environment – are not framed specifically or comparatively, nor do they necessarily reflect strengths investors themselves would cite. Furthermore, there is no explicit connection between Tajikistan's self-assessed strengths and the priority sectors it identifies: industry, energy, transport, and food (Government of Tajikistan, 2012[25]).

IPAs from OECD countries are already prioritising fewer and more focused sectors in response to the pandemic. The changed economic conditions of the pandemic are also generally an opportunity to reassess economic realities and priorities (OECD, 2020[15]). Identifying specific and narrow priority sectors in line with the country's potential and mentioning them consistently should thus become a crucial component of marketing Tajikistan to investors. Once key messages and priority sectors are identified, Tajikistan can use them in more targeted marketing materials and events.

Tajikistan's marketing to investors does not provide specific and consistent messages and information

Tajikistan does not have a strategy for marketing to and targeting investors. Investment promotion action plans usually cover marketing, branding, and targeting of investors through a detailed step-by-step approach. In Tajikistan, the *2012 Concept of State Policy for Attraction and Protection of Investments,* the main investment promotion document to date, does not contain these elements (Government of Tajikistan, 2012[25]; UNCTAD, 2016[26]). Without a strategy to co-ordinate among agencies, Tajikistan's messaging to investors is inconsistent, particularly regarding priority sectors (Box 1).

In the OECD IPA survey, Tajikistan indicated that it conducts a wide range of generalised image-building and marketing activities, spending 20% of its budget thereon, compared to 34% in Eurasia and 18% in OECD countries. These include maintaining multiple websites to promote investment in Tajikistan, making use of international and domestic media, regularly producing promotional materials, and organising public relations events (OECD, 2020[27]).

Tajikistan's main marketing tools to investors are the country's investor guide, which includes generic information on investment opportunities and the investment climate. Other presentations are also available, which tend to be presented at business forums and other investor-related events (UNCTAD, 2016[26]; OECD, 2020[27]). These materials do not provide clear logistical information, which can be further exemplified by Tajikistan's investment promotion websites. These websites, which are often investors' first and primary source of information, are not consistent in their messaging about investment opportunities, and crucial facts are scattered across them (see Box 1). While most sites and media reports emphasise improvements in Tajikistan's business climate (Mirsaidov, 2021[28]) – certainly reassuring for investors – this is merely a prerequisite for investment and does not in itself constitute a valid value proposition. Investors need to be able to find information that helps them determine that Tajikistan is a good location to produce goods or services in a specific industry.

Box 1. An overview of Tajikistan's websites for investors

Tajikistan has a number of investment-related websites. Their strengths include their generally modern appearance and the availability of much content in English as well as Russian, including downloadable information on investment opportunities and legal texts.

- B2b.tj was established by Tajinvest with support from the OSCE and GIZ. Its most useful feature is the detailed information on the legal environment in its "business guide". For example, investors can easily obtain tailored information on exports through an interactive tool that allows a quick search by product and function. However, many pages in this section are not well maintained; the interactive and helpful section "guidelines for investors" was a broken link as of July 2021, and while it is working as of February 2022, it is only available in Russian, even when accessed via the English-language website. The website lists investment projects by general sector, yet it is unclear how regularly these are updated, since the list of projects does not overlap at all with the one provided by the SCISPM on their investment map (map.investcom.tj), nor the list on Tajinvest's main website. The information about each sector includes some basic facts about the sector, numerous priority sub-sectors, and relevant legal incentives but lacks a clear argument for investors about why Tajikistan is a better place to invest in this sector than its competitors. Information about domestic companies, presumably provided for matchmaking purposes, is mostly only available in Russian. News articles are also frequently posted, but there are far more articles in Russian than English.
- Tajinvest.tj is the main website of Tajinvest. It is visually appealing, but it remains unclear how much of the information is still relevant. The priority sectors and investment projects have little overlap with those on the b2b.tj or investcom.tj sites or other government documents (priority sectors are the same as those identified in a 2019 report *Investment Opportunities in Tajikistan,* authored by Tajinvest but available only on the SCISPM website). The section "Why Tajikistan?" is also dated 2019. Detailed information on investment opportunities is only available in a Russian-language downloadable file, whereas b2b.tj has such files available in English. All this suggests that the website has not been updated for the last two years, apart from the news section, which is entirely duplicated on b2b.tj. Since b2b.tj is also co-managed by Tajinvest, it is probably worth consolidating the two websites and eliminating Tajinvest.tj. Despite the government noting digitalisation as its priority in the coming decade, no digital infrastructure project has been listed on the Tajinvest.tj site.
- Investcom.tj is the website of the SCISPM. As the Committee has a variety of mandates, only part of the website is devoted to investment. The specificity of priority sectors compared to the other websites (e.g., beekeeping) is commendable, although other sectors are more general or even encompass the others (e.g., agriculture). The descriptions of these sectors, especially the specific ones, include somewhat better value propositions than the other websites, such as available land and the appropriate native plants for beekeeping. The website also includes a useful map of investment opportunities with fairly detailed information, but these are not the same as those on b2b.tj. Unfortunately, very little of the website appears to be up to date; sections like investor services and priority sector pages were last updated in 2018 according to webpage timestamps. Confusingly, there are two lists of projects, one labelled "priority" and

from 2020, and the other from 2018. The site is somewhat difficult to navigate, as one must return to the homepage to find the section on priority sectors.

- The Ministry of Economic Development and Trade is also actively promoting the Free Economic Zones (FEZ); general information about these is available on the above websites. There is a consolidated page fez.tj. The site provides investors useful information, albeit from 2017 and therefore possibly outdated, on topics like taxes, labour, services, and relevant laws. Investors can also find specific information on websites of each FEZ, with differences in quality and intensity. Supported by UNDP, the MOE is currently developing the websites of individual FEZ, including reference materials to promote them to international investors.

Sources: (SCISPM, TajInvest, GIZ, & OSCE, 2019[29]; SPISPM, 2018[30]; TajInvest, 2019[31]; FEZ "Dangara", 2018[32]; FEZ "Panch" & OSCE, 2009[33])

Tajikistan lacks tools for targeting specific investors

Like its marketing strategy, Tajikistan's approach to targeting investors is expensive yet too general. The SCISPM expends significant resources on general events (sector-specific road shows, business fora, fairs), missions abroad, and one-on-one meetings with prospective investors. It also carries out trade fairs, organises trips for business delegations and signs co-operation agreements with other countries (OECD questionnaire, 2021). Many of the events are co-organised with other government entities. For instance, the Chamber of Commerce and Industry (CCI) regularly organises exhibitions in which the SCISPM takes an active role to follow up with investors if interest arises; more specific agencies, such as the Ministry of Agriculture, participate in events relevant to their work (OECD questionnaire, 2021).

However, the government's investment promotion work does not always target specific countries and investors proactively, an approach with greater likelihood of success and potentially lower costs (OECD, 2020[27]). Instead, most investors had already been present in other Central Asian countries and decided to explore other countries in the region. For instance, Coca Cola is in Tajikistan, Kyrgyzstan, and Kazakhstan. Knowing this, Tajikistan could conduct research on which investors are already present in the region and contact them (see Recommendation 2B). Green energy companies in Kazakhstan like Visor International DMCC and Risen Solar Technology as well as hotel companies in Kyrgyzstan like Novotel and Hyatt Regency may be good fits for Tajikistan's state priority sectors of hydropower and tourism respectively (Agency for the Promotion and Protection of Investments of the Kyrgyz Republic, 2021[34]; Kazakh Invest, 2021[35]).

The SCISPM's co-operation with the network of embassies and consulates could also be further enhanced to carry out effective investor targeting outside of Tajikistan. Over the past years, the visa regime has been simplified, making it easier for investors and individuals alike to request and pay for visas via an electronic channel.

Recommendation 1A: Identify specific target sectors to focus investment promotion efforts

Realistic economic analysis should form the core of Tajikistan's marketing to investors and selection of target sectors

The first step to attracting investors is informing them of opportunities in Tajikistan, through both general marketing and proactive outreach. This, in turn, requires that IPAs identify the country's strengths. Economic realities about development goals or political agendas, must come first if investment attraction is to be realistic and therefore successful (OECD, 2015[36]; WAIPA, 2020[37]; World Bank, 2020[38]). Investors are interested in three major categories of benefits: resources, market, and efficiency. Resource-seeking investors look for environmental features and the labour market, market-seeking look for opportunities to sell their products due to gaps in Tajikistan's domestic production and supply chains, and efficiency-seeking look for low operating costs and other factors that increase efficiency, like specialised human capital (Wadhwa and Reddy, 2011[39]). Ideally, Tajikistan's strengths in each of these areas should be framed with competitors in mind, but in some cases collaboration with neighbours can be more of a benefit than an increased competition from investors' perspective. Collaboration can provide larger markets in the context of Tajikistan and other Central Asian small economies, opportunities for economies of scale, and cross-border infrastructure – including digital (Center for Regional Economic Competitiveness, 2021[40]; Carole Biau, 2015[41]; OECD, 2020[27]). It is also crucial that the value proposition be realistic: it must be based on accurate data and show how Tajikistan's strengths and the IPA's services can compensate for issues in the market or business climate or for gaps with competitors (UN ESCAP, 2019[42]; Clarity Business Strategies, 2018[43]).

Understanding Tajikistan's strengths allows it to identify potentially viable target sectors. Being specific about target sectors is critical to maximising the impact of investment promotion resources, because it enables the IPAs to focus their efforts on sectors that have the best chance of attracting investors and that will bring the most benefit to Tajikistan. According to one study, funds used by an IPA in sector-specific marketing resulted in investments nearly 200 times what the IPA spent (Harding and Javorcik, 2012[44]).

To make an initial list of potential priority sectors, IPAs can use pre-existing analyses and studies, expert opinions, and discussions with current investors (WAIPA, 2020[37]; OECD, 2018[20]). These qualitative data can be supported with quantitative market analysis. Good target sectors are based on a combination of national assets critical to the functioning of the sector; merely one reason to invest in each sector is not enough (Center for Regional Economic Competitiveness, 2021[40]).

Once a list of potential target sectors is created, Tajikistan should conduct a more detailed analysis of the opportunities Tajikistan has in that sector and identify the more narrow sub-sectors that have the greatest potential in Tajikistan. For example, research and analysis could determine if dried fruits, rather than food processing in general, would be a good sector to target based on Tajikistan's comparative advantages (such as high-quality and inexpensive raw fruit inputs). The OECD's *Sector Competitiveness Strategy* for Kazakhstan and the UNCTAD Investment Policy Review of Kyrgyzstan provide examples of market analysis of competitive advantages to choose priority sectors for investment (OECD, 2010[45]; UNCTAD, 2016[46]).

Box 2. Kazakhstan's sector competitiveness strategy

The OECD conducted a thorough sector prioritisation for Kazakhstan in 2010. To make a long list of potential sectors, the OECD started with stakeholder interviews, including government ministries, foreign investors, and BIOs. All sectors were converted to a standardised classification system, namely the Classification of Economic Activities of the European Community NACE. Next, the OECD looked at quantitative data on the economic competitiveness of the sector and benefits for Kazakhstan's development goals. Example economic viability variables included the cost of labour, domestic consumption of the product, and availability of inputs for the production process, including energy demands. Example development attractiveness variables included employment level in the sector, value added per employee, and sector innovation performance index. The sectors that were both most economically viable and beneficial to Kazakhstan were selected. Finally, these findings were reviewed by stakeholders to ensure consideration of qualitative factors that the quantitative analysis may have missed.

One of the sectors identified was Logistics for Agribusiness. This is specific: it refers to a business function within an industry. Detailed analysis of this sector revealed Kazakhstan's concrete value proposition, which would have been even better if it were framed comparatively:

- Central location between Europe and Asia;
- Extensive road and train network;
- Two major logistics centres for warehouses, including a Russian-Kazakh project, and plans to develop a third to improve logistics with China; and
- Doubled value of the logistics sector in Kazakhstan over the past eight years.

At the same time, the strategy was honest about some shortcomings in the sector and the ways that Kazakhstan can address them, which is very important for investors. For instance, the report recommended improved road quality and increased access to refrigerated trucks.

Source: (OECD, 2010[45]).

Specificity about priority narrow sectors, countries, and timeline will maximise the benefits of focused investment promotion

The last step is to select the final sectors reflecting both a unique comparative value proposition and an alignment with development goals (Center for Regional Economic Competitiveness, 2021[40]). The IPA should select no more than 3-5 highly specific sectors (Byrne, 2016[47]; World Bank, 2020[38]). A focus on such specific sectors does not imply that Tajikistan should refuse other FDI opportunities if approached by investors, but rather that resources for proactive investment promotion should be devoted primarily to the priority sectors (World Bank, 2020[38]). Georgia's investment promotion strategy for instance sets out two categories of sectors that it prioritises: (1) priority sectors – sectors that Georgia's IPA actively targets and conducts outreach towards, and (2) facilitation sectors – those in which interest already exists but support is needed to enter the country.

Once sectors are selected, it may be beneficial to focus investment promotion efforts even further on priority countries and projects. Tajikistan already uses a variety of criteria when it comes to project prioritisation, but others could be added to the analysis. Ukraine's IPA, for example, takes into account the investment horizon, and the firm's engagement in internationalisation and the mode of entry. Georgia's IPA uses the size of the company as a criterion too. Both IPAs also focus on priority country of origin (OECD, 2020[27]). For instance, Tajikistan could target South Korea, a recent investor in Tajik cotton textiles (SugdNEWS, 2020[48]). It is also helpful to specify which priority sectors are relevant for which priority countries. This can include considerations of both supply (interests of investors) and demand (benefits for Tajikistan). For instance, on the supply side European countries may be interested in renewable energy, while on the demand side certain Asian countries may be able to provide Tajik manufacturers with desirable high technology (WAIPA, 2020[37]). Investment brochures with comparative value propositions for specific desired projects will help attract investors as well (WAIPA, 2020[37]).

Finally, there may be a need for timeline differentiation depending on targeted sectors. Some may be immediately ready for investment, while others might be part of medium and long-term plans pending reforms. Some IPAs choose to institutionalise these priorities through different subsections or staff responsible for each sector (OECD, 2018[20]). Effective prioritisation over the long term relies on monitoring and evaluation of the quantity and impact of investments in each priority sector, so Tajikistan should be prepared to collect this data (OECD, 2020[15]).

Recommendation 1B: Use digital tools to reduce costs and increase effectiveness

Relatively simple upgrades to IPA websites can easily improve investment attraction

Tajikistan should prioritise consolidation and updating of existing websites. Virtual means of connecting with investors have grown in importance during the pandemic, when in-person interactions became impossible (WAIPA, 2020[37]). An investment-promotion website can be visually quite simple with few graphics and less text, provided it meets the following key criteria: accurate, updated, easily navigable, and translated (UN ESCAP, 2019[42]; Kaymaz, 2019[49]). All content should be in English, and it would be even better if the language of Tajikistan's biggest investor, Chinese, were also an option (Byrne, 2016[47]). Having one investment website is preferable; if there are multiple web sites, care must be taken to ensure that information is consistent across sites. This may entail simplifying and removing less relevant information so that agencies can focus on regular updates (including working hyperlinks) of core content: value proposition, priority sectors, investment opportunities, and logistical information like the legal environment and IPA services. Notably, none of the sites described in Box 1 provided information about COVID-19: this is the kind of core information that investors need.

The content of the website should be driven by consistent messaging about Tajikistan. The front page should clearly state what makes Tajikistan an attractive investment location, and the consistent use of related keywords throughout the website has the additional benefit of helping with search engine optimisation (SEO) (IBT Partners, 2020[50]; Byrne, 2016[47]). Priority sectors – which must be consistent across all government websites – should each have dedicated pages describing individual value propositions, with advantages for each sector (monetised whenever possible), such as land prices and local salaries (OECD, 2018[20]; Clarity Business Strategies, 2018[43]; UN ESCAP, 2019[42]).

Contact information on the website is also critical so that Tajikistan's IPAs can begin direct targeting of individual investors. According to a 2012 report, out of 181 IPAs just 24 (13.3%) responded to inquiries from their websites in a helpful and timely manner (World Bank, 2020[38]). Tajikistan's websites do provide contact information, but this could be improved with more specific contact details regarding individual sectors (WAIPA, 2020[37]). Requesting that site visitors leave some information about themselves can make it easier to follow up. Even if visitors do not leave contact information, site analytics, such as the country of origin of site visitors, can be helpful for targeting purposes.

Box 3. Interactive map of Egypt's investment opportunities is an excellent way to convey information to investors

If time and resources allow, more advanced and interactive tools for the website, like a map, can help investors quickly find information. Currently, the SCISPM hosts an English-only investment project map at map.investcom.tj. This is an excellent step and includes useful features, like filtering by sector. When an investor clicks on a project, they can find further information in English on the project details and incentives. However, lack of co-ordination among agencies means that the investment opportunities featured are not the same as those on b2b.tj or Tajinvest.tj. This raises questions about which – if any – list is up-to-date and thereby relevant to investors. Tajikistan can consider improving its map along the lines of the one hosted by Egypt's IPA.

Egypt's IPA provides a map that summarises important legal information with a geographical component, like zones. This may be particularly useful in Tajikistan's context due to the large number of FEZs that each have their own legal framework and incentives for investors. The Egyptian map also indicates the location of utilities investors may find important, like airports and universities. While

Tajikistan's map directs all interested investors to contact the SCISPM's general email, Egypt's map provides specific, direct contact information of the relevant government entity for that project. The Egyptian map is dynamic and regional officials (or FEZs, in the case of Tajikistan) can easily add new opportunities without waiting for approval from the central IPA, which would ensure the map is continually updated.

Source: (OECD, 2020[51]).

Digital tools can help target specific investors, which is more likely to lead to investment

Generalised image-building, such as through a website, is very important, but successful IPAs also reach out proactively to potential investors in priority sectors (Kaymaz, 2019[49]). This can be viewed as a subsidy for location searches that counteracts investor concerns about additional costs of being a "first mover" in a relatively unknown country like Tajikistan (OECD & Inter-American Development Bank, 2019[21]). Nearly half (47%) of IPAs in OECD countries target specific investors (OECD, 2018[20]).

Before Tajikistan can do this, it needs to make a list of possible investors, a process called lead generation (UN ESCAP, 2019[42]). A first step is ensuring ongoing dialogue with international companies already in Tajikistan, such as Coca Cola, and those that have reached out themselves through the website. Other methods to find companies include sectoral publications, commercial databases such as Hoovers, BIOs, and investors in neighbouring countries. The latter option is especially promising for Tajikistan. Investors could be found through collaborative regional investment forums – including virtual ones with much lower overhead costs for both hosts and investors – that facilitate investment policy co-ordination and highlight potential benefits for investors with a regional dimension like economies of scale, an approach that has been successful in the Southern African Development Community and the Association of Southeast Asian Nations (Byrne, 2016[47]; Kaymaz, 2019[49]; Carole Biau, 2015[41]). Once a list is created, it can be narrowed through basic internet research on each company, including its specific products, market and plant locations, previous investments, and announced future intentions (Kaymaz, 2019[49]). These can then be compared to Tajikistan's value proposition in the sector to determine if Tajikistan fits the investor's needs.

It is also helpful to consider potential investors as customers and include them in a CRM system like SalesForce even before they choose to invest. This allows the IPA to keep track of their contact information over time and contact them about customised future opportunities for investment as they become available (Loewendahl and Bryan, 2019[52]). The IPA should set specific objectives for the frequency and timeline of communication with potential investors and engage in "politely persistent" outreach to high-level company executives (Caribbean Export Development Agency, 2014[53]; Kaymaz, 2019[49]). Such a database has advantages for communicating with current investors as well; IPAs with CRM systems could communicate with and support current and potential investors about changing conditions related to the pandemic (OECD, 2020[15]).

Once an investor is closely considering a project in Tajikistan, digital tools can help make the decision. A standard online library of important documents and clear operating procedures for IPA staff members can ensure responses are quick (World Bank, 2020[38]). Videoconferences and virtual site visits, and digital trade and economic missions may be necessary as the pandemic continues and useful afterwards as well since they are less costly for both the investor and IPA (OECD, 2020[51]).

A long-term approach to relationships with potential investors is necessary, since it might take years for the right project and timing to emerge, and even then investment decisions are a lengthy process (WAIPA, 2020[37]). Not everything about the investment targeting process can or should be digitised. Building trust and partnerships with potential investors through personal contact complements robust CRM and accurate, useful online information (Tsimal, 2020[54]). To add a human dimension to the digital tools, assigning individual staff members as account managers for designated prospective investors provides consistency (OECD, 2018[20]). Recruiting the right staff to carry out marketing and branding activities will be a critical priority in the years ahead, particularly ensuring the advanced digital skills needed to promote Tajikistan as an investment destination (UNCTAD, 2016[26]; OECD, 2020[27]).

Recommendation 2. Strengthen the institutional setting and strategy of investment promotion

Challenge: The institutional setting behind investment promotion is complex

Actors with overlapping and numerous mandates undertake investment promotion in Tajikistan

Tajikistan has one main body involved in investment promotion, and several other government bodies that also have roles to play in this field. Investment promotion is primarily in the hands of the SCISPM, which is responsible for the design and implementation of investment policy, and Tajinvest, a state unitary enterprise supervised by the SCISPM. At the same time, it is the Ministry of Economic Development and Trade that designs policies related to free economic zones (FEZ), which are part of the investment promotion system. It is also the same Ministry that conducts FEZ-specific investment promotion activities, such as organising events and roundtables with investors to which it invites the SCISPM and Tajinvest. Similarly, the Ministry of Finance and the Ministry of Industry and Innovative Technologies, alongside business associations, organise investment promotion events that seek to attract investment in their sectors. Like FEZs, regional investment promotion bodies occasionally help organise promotion events and assist investors in their dedicated regions. To conduct policy advocacy and support public-private dialogue on investment, the government has also put in place the Consultative Council on Improvement of Investment Climate, which the SCISPM chairs.

The SCISPM currently has 12 mandates, which is more than the average number of mandates of agencies in charge of investment promotion in Eurasia (6.5) and the OECD (5.7) (OECD, 2020[27]). Besides foreign investment promotion, the SCISPM is responsible for managing state enterprises, privatisation, supporting SMEs and entrepreneurship, and, since 2018, hosting a business incubator. Tajinvest is charged more narrowly with investment promotion, but in practice currently primarily provides business development services (BDS) to domestic companies (Tajinvest, 2021; OECD interviews, 2021).

The SCISPM is the parent agency, and it has significantly greater statutory powers. According to its government-approved charter, it plays a leading role in designing investment policy, independently negotiates agreements with investors, provides all necessary documents and permissions for investors through a single-window system, defends the legal interests of investors, proactively attracts investments, and co-ordinates investments with other government agencies (Government of the Republic of Tajikistan, 2006[55]).Tajinvest is only able to advise investors (on legal aspects, tax legislation, operational and business issues) and implement policies adopted by the SCISPM. Investors are under the impression that the SCISPM is responsible for public investment, whereas Tajinvest handles private investment, but this distinction is not enshrined in law and indeed contradicts the SCISPM's mandate to attract and assist *all* investors (OECD interviews, 2021).

Organisational reforms may have contributed to this confusion about mandates and tasks. While the allocation of roles and responsibilities may be clear to officials in the relevant bodies, investors report being unsure about, for example, whom to contact in legislative matters related to their investments. The SCISPM, established in 2006, has gone through five reorganisations in the past ten years. These have involved additional mandates, particularly the mandate to be a single-window as of 2017. While it is critical that investment promotion institutions adapt to a changing policy environment, a measure of institutional stability is essential to reducing confusion among investors and effective long-term planning. Responses to the OECD IPA survey show that organisational reforms are rather common in Eurasia, reflecting changes in government and the need to adapt to new economic realities. It is thus no surprise that IPAs in Eurasia see "the instability or inadequacy of their mandates" as their number one challenge (OECD, 2020[27]).

While the SCISPM's many mandates, from privatisation to SME development, may bear synergies with investment promotion, it is important to ensure that the resources allocated to the SCISPM match its diverse and broad responsibilities. Tajinvest has increasingly shifted its focus towards supporting domestic business development (trainings, advisory services), activities that are financially more promising but still generate insufficient income to ensure the capacity to reach out to investors and promote the country effectively (UNCTAD, 2016[26]).

In addition, Tajikistan could benefit greatly from improvements in the skills and experience of IPA employees, especially private-sector experience. Staff with a public sector background comprise 87% of SCISPM and Tajinvest (Figure 6), which may affect the Committee's capabilities in areas where private-sector experience is an advantage (UNCTAD, 2016[26]; OECD, 2020[27]). Level of experience and length of tenure also matter. Interviews indicated that staff turnover is high, affecting the ease with which staff can build relationships with investors and ensure continuity of the activities. The interviews also suggest that salary levels may contribute to high turnover and make recruitment from the private sector harder. Tajik government stakeholders rank inadequate staff as a major challenge (OECD, 2020[27]). Recruitment mechanisms may also need to be considered; it may be useful to advertise opportunities in non-governmental job forums.

Figure 6. Staff profiles across Eurasia's IPAs

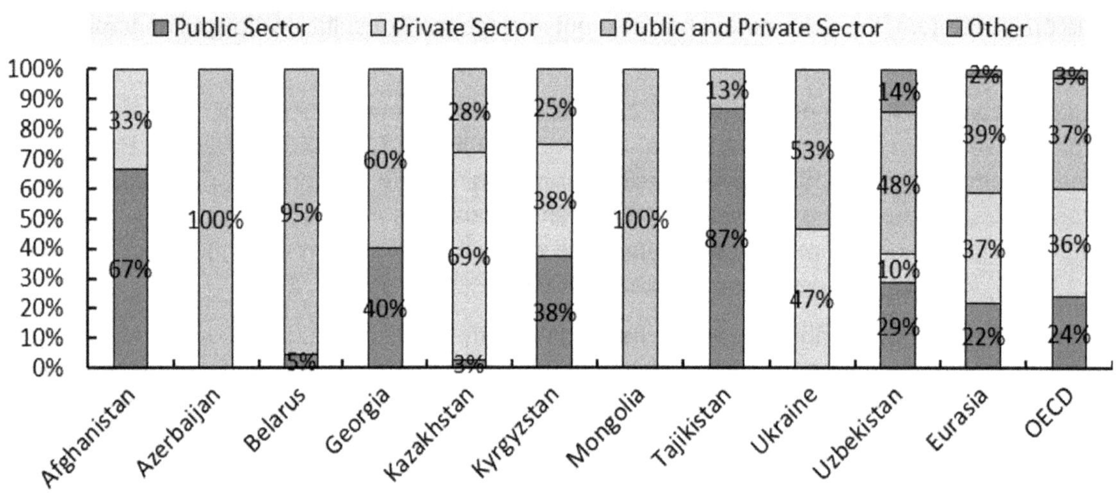

Source: (OECD, 2020[27])

Tajikistan needs an integrated, broad-based investment promotion strategy

At present, Tajikistan does not have an updated investment promotion strategy. The most recent government strategy for investment is the *2012 Concept of Government Policy for Attraction and Protection of Investments*. Despite its name, it is not an investment promotion strategy *per se*, since it does not outline and co-ordinate activities of the IPAs. Instead, it is a broader statement of issues with and plans to improve the investment climate. The Concept identifies issues such as poor infrastructure, small internal market, large bureaucracy, and emigration of qualified workers. It commits Tajikistan to continuing a path of improving the investment climate and attracting more FDI, including clear "rules of the game", greater transparency, less government interference in the private sector through minimised bureaucratic hurdles, reduced corruption, consolidating and harmonising the legal environment, instituting a mechanism for resolving disputes with investors, and protecting their rights through a stronger judicial system (OECD, 2021[2]).

The SCISPM does not have the mandate to assign roles to other institutions in charge of promoting investment. It prepares only annual plans for its own work, which cannot provide needed co-ordination among relevant agencies (Government of the Republic of Tajikistan, 2006[55]).

Recommendation 2A: Clarify institutional responsibilities, accountability, and resources to avoid confusion and inefficiencies

Tajikistan should clarify the roles and mandates of institutions active in investment promotion

Tajikistan's laws related to investment promotion and the charters of its IPAs require harmonisation, to take account of recent changes. Government-approved amendments to the SCISPM's charters could better align its powers with the specifics of current legislation and distinguish the agencies' tasks more clearly. For this process, Tajikistan should prepare a checklist of licences, permissions, incentives and permits required to invest and operate a foreign-owned business, and decide which powers to grant to the IPA (OECD, 2015[36]). The key is to ensure that IPAs are not *another* bureaucratic hurdle for investors but rather *ease* bureaucratic requirements by making the responsibilities of each agency clear. Most Eurasia IPAs have single windows for investor services, so more direct service provision would bring Tajikistan in line with regional peers (OECD, 2020[27]).

Reforms to the legal and institutional environment for investment promotion should be considered carefully to ensure stability and avoid such contradictions in the future. Continuous institutional change can create confusion for investors, who do not know with whom they should interact (OECD, 2020[27]). This, in turn, damages long-term relationships, which are the key to successful FDI attraction. Therefore, it is recommended that Tajikistan make changes with a medium-term vision and develop plans clearly to communicate changes to investors.

SCISPM needs sufficient independence and resources to carry out their mandates

When strategic decision-making and reporting are necessary, they should be done at the highest level. Interactions with many other government agencies, while sometimes helpful in synergising work and adopting a whole-of-government approach, can also divert scarce resources from core IPA functions (OECD, 2020[27]). This is common in Eurasia. Minimising reporting requirements to intermediaries, while establishing strong communication channels with the country's top decision makers – especially since IPA-government linkages are strong throughout Eurasia and specifically in Tajikistan – will allow for efficient operation and needed political visibility (OECD, 2020[27]; OECD, 2015[36]). In this connection, the fact that the SCISPM chair is a presidential appointee could well be seen as an advantage for Tajikistan.

International experience shows that agencies with operational autonomy, including the freedom to set objectives and allocate their budgets, tend to be more effective. Public funding frees IPAs from the burden of self-financing, but annual requests for funding mean that their work is subject to short-term political and economic circumstances, undermining the capacity to implement long-term plans. One solution would be to allocate funding for multiple years within the country's medium-term expenditure framework, allowing agencies to make long-term plans for their own budgets and delineate expenses in accordance with their mandates, as is the case of Invest in Georgia (Box 4). It should be noted that such budgetary independence would require revisiting the legal status of the SCISPM, as the level of autonomy described would be difficult to reconcile with its status as a budgetary organisation. Tajikistan would have to consider many factors in reaching any such decision, but the critical priority should be to ensure adequate, stable and predictable resourcing for investment promotion.

Box 4. Invest in Georgia

Invest in Georgia is part of a broader government economic development agency – Enterprise Georgia. The agency operates under the Ministry of Economy and Sustainable Development of Georgia and beyond FDI attraction, it is also responsible for SME development and export promotion. The aim of Invest in Georgia division is to attract, promote and develop foreign direct investments in Georgia. It serves as a "one-stop-shop" for investors, to support companies before, during and after the investment process (this legal mandate is reflected in the corresponding law). The division plays the role of a facilitator between foreign investors and the Government of Georgia, ensuring that the investor receives relevant updated information and can communicate with the different Government bodies.

In order to undertake these responsibilities, the Invest in Georgia division (as well as Enterprise Georgia) receives a pre-approved annual budget, based on a pre-developed action plan. Accordingly, the agency executes the activities and utilizes the budget without further need of approval on behalf of the Ministry or other parties. With this, the agency has developed a two-year FDI promotion strategy and action plan (alongside specific KPIs), which was approved by the Ministry of Economy and Sustainable Development (first approved in 2020 and updated in 2021) and the agency is correspondingly responsible for its implementation.

For policy-making purposes in terms of FDI, the Ministry of Economy and Sustainable Development of Georgia also operates a special department – the Investment Policy and Support Department. The Invest in Georgia division, also works closely with the Department to promote/lobby for certain policy level adjustments or changes, when such are required.

Source: Enterprise Georgia

International experience suggests that strong private-sector participation in an IPA can enable a better understanding of private-sector needs and facilitate public-private dialogue (OECD, 2015[36]). In addition to recruiting staff with private-sector experience, this can include bringing private-sector representatives into the supervisory board. More flexibility and autonomy in salary-setting, which is an aspect of institutional independence, could make it easier to recruit the needed staff, particularly for specific roles where high-demand qualifications are required (OECD, 2020[27]). Recruitment mechanisms may also need to be reconsidered; it may be useful to advertise opportunities in non-governmental job forums.

Box 5. Kazakh Invest Legal Authority and Mandate

Kazakh Invest was established with a strong legal foundation, a government resolution adopted on 1 March 2017. The government approves the IPA's overarching strategy, but the agency also has an independent supervisory board, which oversees planning and budgeting. Kazakh Invest has the clear authority and mandate to attract investment and provide full range of services to investors from an initial idea to implementation as well as during post-investment period. In its own words, it is:

- a unified negotiator on behalf of the Government of the Republic of Kazakhstan in discussing the prospects and conditions for the implementation of investment projects; and
- a "single window" to the system of public services for investors, including the provision of measures of state support to investors in the form of investment preferences and incentives, and, assistance in obtaining various permits and approvals required for the implementation and further operation of investment projects.

* Resolution of the Government of the Republic of Kazakhstan No. 100, "On the renaming of the National Export and Investment Agency KAZNEX INVEST Joint-Stock Company in order to promote sustainable socio-economic development of the Republic of Kazakhstan by attracting foreign investment in priority sectors of the economy and comprehensive support of investment projects", 1 March 2017.
Source: (Kazakh Invest, 2021[56]).

Recommendation 2B: Create a strategic framework with well-defined, actionable objectives and methods to co-ordinate the work of IPAs

Tajikistan needs an updated and more detailed investment promotion strategy

Investment promotion in Tajikistan requires clear and co-ordinated objectives and administrative procedures to achieve results and value for money. This is why Tajikistan should adopt an investment promotion strategy that identifies its objectives and available financial and human resources. Given limited resources for IPAs' activities, a clear and specific strategy can help ensure their efficient use (OECD, 2020[27]). Such a strategy, if underpinned by concrete actions plans for individual agencies and an adequate monitoring and evaluation framework, could help ensure that investment promotion activities are well-co-ordinated and achieve intended results.

While the 2012 Concept includes some valuable goals, many of which are still relevant, Tajikistan's post-pandemic circumstances make the development of an updated, more specific strategy critical. The changed global conditions after COVID-19 require a fresh assessment of goals, opportunities, and methods (OECD, 2020[27]). Developing a strategy is a perfect opportunity to analyse new economic conditions and make a plan to adapt.

Well-designed investment promotion strategies co-ordinate all investment promotion activity in a country. While the IPA is at the centre of investment promotion and therefore the centre of the strategic process, the strategy can and should extend to investment-related activities of other agencies, so that the government has a unified approach and can streamline activities and uses resources efficiently. In the Tajik context, this means that an investment strategy developed by the SCISPM should cover Tajinvest and the FDI-related activities of other agencies, such as the Ministry of Economic Development and Trade.

Strategies should articulate specific goals and objectives for the IPA as well as the methods and resources it will use to achieve them; goals, resources, and methods must align for the strategy to be effective (OECD, 2020[27]). The document answers four essential questions: *why* the country needs investment, *who* and *what* priority sectors to target for investment, and specifically *how* the IPA and other institutions will do this (OECD, 2015[36]; OECD, 2020[51]). It also covers the indicators that will be used to measure performance and evaluate impact. Strategies are based on considerations of both supply – what Tajikistan can *offer* investors – and demand – what investors *want* from Tajikistan (Loewendahl and Bryan, 2019[52]). They are clear, specific, distinct from other countries' strategies, and internally consistent (OECD, 2015[36]).

International experience suggests that investment promotion strategies are successful when they are given due time and attention, which is why Tajikistan should not rush the process. Strategies must be adapted to the country's situation, as demonstrated in the *Mapping of Investment Promotion Agencies in OECD Countries*, as the evidence suggests that different activities, approaches and strategies are suitable for different agencies, even in broadly similar economic contexts (OECD, 2018[20]). Setting objectives for target sectors and countries requires extensive market research. The research process should also include consultations with a wide range of stakeholders, especially representatives of the private sector. This is a time-consuming but critical endeavour (Caribbean Export Development Agency, 2014[53]). IPAs may also want to receive advice from international development organisations and companies (Millenium Cities Initiative, 2009[57]). There are a number of online resources that can be helpful as well, such as the World Bank and WAIPO websites. The first step in the process is therefore formulating a plan for development of the strategy: designating the manager, allocating staff, and creating a timeframe for the completion of strategy components (Caribbean Export Development Agency, 2014[53]).

Since policy level decisions and actions are relatively harder to implement and take significant time to be reviewed, there could be a case for developing two strategies at once: one focusing on the improvements needed on the policy level to smoothen the general investment climate and a second focused on promotion and hands-on activities of the investment promotion agencies. This approach could save time, and allow the investment agency to strategically and actively promote investment offers in parallel to policy level changes being undertaken though a separate more intensive and time consuming process.

Clear, evidence-based objectives and corresponding monitoring and evaluation mechanisms can help ensure the strategy achieves intended results

The next step is to articulate *why* Tajikistan needs FDI. A strategy should contain mission and vision statements that are short and connected to Tajikistan's unique overall development goals (Loewendahl and Bryan, 2019[52]). For example, two overarching goals that frequently reoccur in Tajik legal and strategic documents are creating jobs and diversifying the economy, so the mission and vision statement should connect to these and other principles identified as top priority. While many outcomes may be desirable, such as regional development, increasing competition, and expanding, it is important to focus on the *most* important reasons why more FDI would be beneficial to Tajikistan. The mission and vision for the IPA allows the country to articulate specific goals and objectives for the agency. These are measurable and attached to a particular timeframe (Box 6) (Loewendahl and Bryan, 2019[52]). Moreover, articulating such goals clearly is likely to draw attention to other policies that may need to be adjusted in order for FDI, if attracted, to yield its full benefits, for example policies to support linkages with domestic firms, avoid FDI-financed enclave economies, and foster productivity and skills spill-overs from foreign to local firms.

Box 6. Goals and objectives of the IDA Ireland

The 2021-2024 FDI strategy of Ireland's IPA, IDA Ireland, is an excellent example of agenda-setting.

IDA identified five overarching goals, which it calls pillars, that reflect the development priorities of Ireland in the post-pandemic context:

- Under the growth pillar, IDA will win investment to support job creation and economic activity.
- Under the transformation pillar, IDA will partner with clients for future growth in Ireland.
- Under the regions pillar, IDA will win investment to advance regional development.

- Under the sustainability pillar, IDA will embrace an inclusive and green recovery.
- Under the impact pillar, IDA will maximise FDI's positive impact on local businesses and communities.

IDA set the specific, measurable objectives for 2021-2024 in line with its five pillars:

- Win 800 total investments to support job creation of 50,000 and economic activity;
- Partner with clients for future growth through 170 RD&I and 130 training investments;
- Win 400 investments to advance regional development;
- Embrace the opportunities of a green recovery with 60 sustainability investments; and
- Target a 20% increase in client expenditure in Ireland to maximize the impact of FDI.

Source: (IDA Ireland, 2021[58])

A strategy is a living document and needs consistent monitoring to ensure its continued effectiveness and relevance. As conditions and goals change over time, the strategy should change as well. The best strategies incorporate plans for monitoring performance, including mechanisms to solicit feedback from investors (such as through a customer relationship management system (CRM), detailed in Recommendation 1B and continuous dialogue, detailed in Recommendation 3) and the indicators that will be collected, *from the outset* (Loewendahl and Bryan, 2019[52]). It makes no sense to design monitoring and evaluation systems *ex post*. It is important that indicators be limited, such that they are manageable to collect given the IPA's numerous responsibilities, and meaningful, meaning they focus on how well the IPA's methods achieve its economic goals rather than inputs (OECD, 2020[27]). This data collection allows the IPA to serve as an advocate for investors, promoting policies that will improve the business climate (see Recommendation 3) and increase transparency about public spending, particularly important during crises when finances are constrained (OECD, 2020[27]). Using this monitoring and evaluation, the strategy should be reviewed and updated every 3 to 5 years (Caribbean Export Development Agency, 2014[53]).

An actionable strategy needs clarity about targets, methods, resources, and roles

Broad goals and objectives are a starting point for understanding in *what* areas the IPA aims to attract investment. However, extensive research is also necessary to ensure the strategy is realistic and determine whom to target for investment. The developers of the strategy should create a SWOT (Strengths, Weaknesses, Opportunities and Threats) chart for the country based on comparative advantages and disadvantages, benchmarking against neighbours and other countries with similar endowments (Loewendahl and Bryan, 2019[52]). The chart should be developed through intra-agency brainstorming, interviews with stakeholders like current investors, and quantifiable data (Caribbean Export Development Agency, 2014[53]). Strengths and opportunities are what the IPA can highlight to potential investors, and awareness of weaknesses and threats can allow the agency to develop risk mitigation plans and reassure investors. Combined with the country's goals, the SWOT analysis helps the IPA to identify promising sectors and cross-sector business functions that match Tajikistan's strengths (Millenium Cities Initiative, 2009[57]). Sector and business functions allow the strategy developers to identify *who* is likely to invest, in terms of both countries and individual companies (see Recommendation 1 for more detail on defining a value proposition and identifying target sectors and investors). In Georgia for instance, the investment agency undertook a sector scanning exercise, which took into consideration both global trends, as well as Georgia's value propositions and unique selling points. This allowed for the selection of priority sectors in terms of two larger criteria: *desirability* – what does the Government want to get from FDI – and *feasibility* – which sectors have the realistic potential to develop in Georgia.

Finally, the strategy should clarify exactly *how* Tajikistan will conduct investment promotion and facilitation, including which agencies perform what roles, what methods will be employed, and how the strategy will be resourced over its lifespan. As noted above, provision for monitoring, evaluation and adjustment is also critical. Monitoring and evaluation exercises serve little purpose if they do not feed back into policy making to improve the overall investment climate, allowing for timely adjustment of plans and activities.

Recommendation 3. Better leverage the policy advocacy function and improve the facilitation system

Challenge: Investors struggle with the *de facto* investment climate and do not receive enough facilitation and advocacy support from Tajikistan's IPAs

Tajikistan's legal framework for investment facilitation is relatively strong, but resources could be better spent

In 2016, the government introduced a new Law on Investment (LoI) that codifies investment procedures and guarantees a number of investor rights and protections (Government of Tajikistan, 2016[59]). Many of these are in line with investment policy good practices, including:

- non-discrimination and equality before the law for foreign and domestic investors (Art. 7), including the opportunity to participate in privatisation (Art. 12);
- stability of the legal environment, such that if a law worsening investment conditions is adopted, investors do not have to comply for 10 years (excepting laws on national security, health, the environment or morality (Art. 8);
- protection from direct expropriation; a definition of indirect expropriation and provisions for compensation (Art. 14);
- freedom to repatriate profits (Art. 10) and property, including intellectual property, in accordance with customs law (Art. 16) and to convert currency (Art. 11); and
- free access to all relevant legal information for investors in an online format (Art. 13).

The LoI is supplemented by the 2012 *Law on Investment Agreements*, the 2011 *Law on Free Economic Zones*, and the charters of the SCISPM and Tajinvest. Taken together, they provide the legal framework for international investment and a relatively strong set of guarantees for investors.

Information on relevant legislation has become more easily accessible, but issues remain

Many investment-related laws and policy documents can be found across different websites and are often available only in Russian or Tajik. Investors must purchase access to *Adliya*, a commercial legal database, to obtain updated legal and regulatory information.

Efforts to increase transparency and access to information through systematising digital delivery of investment-related legislation is already underway. The SCISPM has created a B2B Business Portal that integrates information from eight government agencies, including the tax portal (which itself has implemented a notable digitalisation campaign) and the National Bank of Tajikistan. This portal is a significant improvement, with key pieces of legislation available in English, Russian and Tajik. Investors can also find key legislation in these languages on the SCISPM and Tajinvest websites.

However, updates appear to be irregular. Most notably, during the COVID-19 pandemic the SCISPM and Tajinvest have not added new legal information that is important to investors, such as information on lockdowns, tax measures, and credit support (Blavatnik School of Government, 2020[60]). Despite the clear consequences of these for investors and the private sector more broadly, information on the pandemic and crisis response is limited to the website of the Ministry of Health (OECD questionnaire, 2021). Investors say that this caused uncertainty on their end. In the context of lingering uncertainty over the impact of COVID-19 on the country's economy, it is more crucial than ever to ensure that investors have access to reliable and updated information.

Tajikistan's IPAs have a legal mandate to facilitate investment facilitation, but they are trying to do too much with too little

On average, Eurasia IPAs devote fewer resources to investment facilitation and retention than other regions: 17% compared to 30% in OECD countries. In contrast, the SCISPM devotes 30% of its budget to investment facilitation and 30% to policy advocacy, a percentage matched only by Kazakhstan and Ukraine in Eurasia (OECD questionnaire, 2021) (OECD, 2020[27]). However, this figure is relative to the overall resources at the SCISPM's disposal, so Tajikistan devotes fewer resources than its neighbours in absolute terms. With these limited resources, the State Committee aims to provide a long list of investment facilitation and aftercare functions[4]. This raises questions about how much the country can devote to each facilitation activity (OECD, 2020[27]).

Policy advocacy institutions aimed at improving the investment climate are relatively robust, but their impact is unclear

To support public-private dialogue on investment, the government has established the Consultative Council on Improvement of the Investment Climate. The Council prepares recommendations for the President and the government on matters related to private sector development and the investment climate (UNCTAD, 2016[26]). It is chaired by the President himself and includes four permanent representatives (the Prime Minister, the First Deputy Prime Minister, the Chair of the SCISPM – who acts as its Executive Secretary – and the Head of the Council Secretariat), seventeen rotating representatives: three from development partners, and 14 members from the private sector (13 domestic businesses and one foreign investor). Tajikistan developed the platform in 2007 with support from the international donor community starting with sub-national PPD mechanisms (Kosymova and Abdujabborov, 2015[61]). In the OECD IPA survey, Tajikistan indicated that it spends 30% of its budget on policy advocacy, compared to 12% in Eurasia and 6% in OECD countries. (Consultative Council on Improvement of Investment Climate under the President of the Republic of Tajikistan, 2021[62]).

The main meetings of the Council are chaired by the Chairman of the Council, the President or the First Deputy Prime Minister (an intersessional meeting of the Council). Topics and issues for discussion at Council meetings are proposed by the private sector, then, in the filtering process, the main topics for discussion at the Council meeting are selected. The Secretariat of the Council conducts analyses on selected topics and prepares recommendations with the participation of representatives of the private sector, experts and industry business associations. After discussion at a meeting of the Council, on the basis of recommendations, a draft action plan for individual sectors is developed. The Council produces annual monitoring reports, with the most recent available report from March 2020. The report demonstrates that, for the most part, the government assigns the Council or one of its ministry members (frequently the SCISPM) the development of a particular policy proposal or action plan, which is then returned to the government for review and possible approval (Consultative Council on Improvement of Investment Climate under the President of the Republic of Tajikistan, 2020[63]).

These arrangements are meant to enable investors to put policy issues on the agenda or make concrete contributions to the policy proposals. It is unclear, though, how many of these proposals ultimately become law, or the timeframes in which they do so. While the Council is not designed as a platform for individual investors to state specific grievances (as opposed to addressing broader policy concerns), occasionally such issues are on the agenda, such as a request for land from the domestic chicken processing company Behamto, cited in the 2019 monitoring report.

Other mechanisms for PPD exist as well. According to an OECD survey, the Chamber of Commerce and Industry of Tajikistan – the country's largest business association – and smaller business intermediary organisations (BIOs) participate quarterly in a variety of government councils and working groups. Of particular note is the current working group on reforming the tax code, as described in Box 8.

Box 7. Tajikistan's new tax code

In 2019, the Tax Committee and Ministry of Finance initiated a reform of the tax code, in order to align it with international best practice, and to adapt it to new realities for businesses and individuals. The new version reduces the number of taxes from 10 to 7, introduces measures intended to improve tax administration and reduces the rates of a number of specific taxes, including VAT. There are preferential tax regimes for a number of sectors.[5]

The new tax code also aims to limit unplanned inspections and audits, as new technologies and risk management tools are used to identify tax violations, rendering it unnecessary to conduct additional unplanned inspections. The number of inspections has in any case been declining gradually in recent years. With the new code, individuals will also be able to submit tax returns electronically, which is meant to reduce compliance costs (especially in terms of time). Since 2012, the Tax Committee has been providing digital services on andoz.tj; it now provides sixty services for legal entities, individual entrepreneurs, individuals, civil servants, government agencies and the banking sector.

The new code was developed by an interdepartmental working group. It took into account numerous comments and proposals from ministries and departments, the private sector and the development community. The committee consulted international financial institutions such as the World Bank, the IMF, the Asian Development Bank, and the EBRD.

Source: Tax Committee; Ministry of Finance

Investors in Tajikistan struggle with bureaucratic requirements despite recent reforms

Despite a range of recent reforms (Box 9), administrative burdens remain an issue for many investors. As described in detail in the OECD's recent *Improving the Legal Environment for Business in Central Asia* report, despite the relatively good formal legal framework, implementation gaps sometimes undermine the quality, transparency, and coherence of the investment process (OECD, 2021[2]). Investors highlighted what they see as inconsistent interpretation and arbitrary application of investment laws, which hinder the process of transparent investing (OECD interviews, 2021). Therefore, Tajikistan's investors need IPA support with investment logistics and continued policy advocacy to address remaining bottlenecks in legislation, public administration and the judicial system (OECD, 2021[2]).

Box 8. Tajikistan's recent legal and regulatory reforms to improve the investment climate

The Tajik government has undertaken a series of reforms to bring the investment climate in line with international standards, including:

- **Business registration**: the government has introduced the opportunity to digitally register a business or pay taxes, by using national payment cards, along with a centralised electronic registry for movable property.
- **Inspections**: the government adopted a new edition of the *Law on Inspections* that makes it mandatory for inspection bodies to report all inspections of businesses digitally. This information is then relayed to a newly established *Co-ordination Council of Inspection Bodies* and a special website in order to keep track of them.
- **Banking and Access to finance**: New amendments to the *Law on Credit History* have expanded the coverage of credit bureaus from 15.9% to 47.6% of the adult population between 2016 and 2020, thereby strengthening the protection of the rights of lenders and borrowers. Moreover, the government has aimed to strengthen the legislative base for secure transactions and the bankruptcy in order to reinforce creditors and borrowers' legal rights.
- **Competition**: the government launched an electronic portal for public procurement. The corresponding by-laws are being developed to better adapt it to the needs of SMEs.
- **Commercial justice**: the Supreme Economic Court, the economic court of Dushanbe, Khatlon region, Sughd region and of GBAO have launched their websites to facilitate the access for citizens and businesses, to legislative and judicial information. Users can also find helplines, and a feedback platform. In addition, a recent package of bills[6] strengthened the rights of creditors and simplified the process of resolving insolvency.
- **Real Estate**: the "single window" to register real estate digitally has been established, thereby merging five government departments in one.
- **Trade**: Tajikistan's Trade Portal, an online platform with descriptions of import and export procedures has been launched. The government is also testing a pilot "single window for the registration of transit and export-import" which unites ten licensing authorities for trade related purposes.

Source: SCISPM, Tax Committee, Ministry of Finance.

Investors want greater facilitation support

Investors tend to see investment screening mechanisms, including into Free Economic Zones (FEZ), as an impediment. The SCISPM oversees the screening process, which can be lengthy and, in the view of investors, opaque. In the absence of clear information about requirements, investors may be inclined to use personal connections with senior government officials. This may lead to decisions that favour market incumbents and reduce pressure to improve the transparency and consistency of the investment regime (OECD, 2021[2]). Even the *perception* that this may happen can be sufficient to deter some investors.

There are several useful but limited digital services for investors from other agencies. Investors can apply for a business (K) e-visa for 60 days, but cannot electronically apply for the specialised investor (C) visa (Ministry of Foreign Affairs, 2021[64]). Registered users of the "Customs Service Single Window" can digitally complete 22 export and import-related transactions, although this is only available in Tajik and Russian (Customs Service, 2021[65]; SCISPM & TajInvest, 2020[66]). The Tax Committee provides a range of digital filing and payment services, which enjoy very high satisfaction and usage from Tajik citizens

(OECD questionnaire of the State Tax Committee, 2021). The tax committee's website offers services in Russian, English and Tajik, although the documents that need to be completed mostly remain in Tajik. The explanatory and informational resources of the Tax Committee website are regularly updated and translated into English. In addition, a contact centre can put individuals in contact with the International Co-operation Office, whose specialists speak Russian, English, French, Chinese and Japanese. While the main page of the Tax Committee has now been translated to English, the documents and subsequent explanations remain in Tajik and Russian (Tax Committee, 2021[67]). In 2021, the website of the Tax Committee - andoz.tj recorded more than 137 000 visits from outside Tajikistan, including 6004 visits from the USA, 1836 from the UK, 2924 from the Netherlands, 1637 from Germany, 1865 from China, 93049 visits from Russia and 30334 visits from other countries.

The SCISPM is aware of the importance of digitalising investor services and is committed to improving them. In response to an OECD questionnaire, the Committee identified China's IPA, China Council for the Promotion of International Trade, as the example of digital services it wishes to emulate. The Invest China website provides various services such as registration, accounting, and licencing for registered users (Investment Promotion Center of CCPIT, 2021[68]).

Investors already in the country could benefit from stronger IPA support

Investors interviewed for this report described limited support during their investor journey, especially when they encountered issues relating to the implementation of guarantees in the LoI and their investor agreements. Investors who feel they receive inadequate support or believe they are not able to secure the conditions they believed were offered may refrain from future investment or even share their negative assessments with other potential investors (OECD interviews, 2021). While individualised intervention is not necessarily typical of all IPAs, Tajikistan's environment and the SCISPM's mandate to support investors with legal issues would seem to warrant such a role.

Investors cite numerous issues that would benefit from IPA intervention, particularly with respect to property, inspections and taxation (OECD, 2021[2]). Protection against, and regulation of, expropriation of private property is captured in the 2016 LoI, and most cases of expropriation concern procedural or criminal violations in privatisations. However, investors have cited cases in which they claimed to have been denied access to infrastructure essential for business operations, which may constitute indirect expropriation. Some investors also complained of unplanned inspections (sanitary/ standard/ anti-monopoly/ fire department), despite a 2018 moratorium on such inspections in production facilities, except for inspections by tax officials, prosecutors, the audit chamber, anticorruption officials and the National Bank (Eurasianet, 2018[69]).

Enforcement of tax laws is a major concern cited by investors. The Tax Committee notes that additional tax incentives have been established for investors within the framework of investment agreements in recent years. Agreements signed with more than 18 investors and executors of investment projects exempt them from income tax and social tax for non-residents for set periods (up to ten years). When importing equipment and spare parts, they may be exempt from value added tax and customs duties. In addition, there are other investment agreements, according to which investors and executors of investment projects are completely exempt from paying all taxes, except for income and social tax for residents for up to 10 years. Some investors have raised concerns that these exemptions may not work in practice and that they "cannot access or utilise most of these incentives" (U.S. Department of State, 2020[70]). However, the Tax Committee emphasises that it has received no complaints from investors about failure to honour these tax preferences and that the volume of such tax incentives has risen over time, from TJS 2.1 billion in 2015 to TJS 3.9 billion in 2019.

Although some businesses have included clauses in bilateral investment treaties (BITs) that mandate the use of international courts for dispute resolution and Tajikistan is a signatory to the 1958 New York

Convention, some observers report encountering problems with domestic courts' implementation of foreign arbitration awards and domestic contract enforcement (Santander Trade, 2021[17]) (OECD, 2021[2]).

There is no department responsible for relations with existing or prospective new investors and no database or customer relationship management (CRM) system in which their contact information is stored (see Recommendation 2B). In this context, limited investor aftercare is carried out, potentially affecting important re-investment opportunities. The SCISPM is aware of the issue and stated that it plans to improve and digitise monitoring and data collection in an OECD questionnaire.

Therefore, requesting support from SCISPM can be complicated, and in interviews some investors complained about a lack of response from the Committee to inquiries. According to its website, the SCISPM will not provide services to investors without six required documents, including a certificate of state registration, charter of the company, and an official, stamped letter requesting the service (SCISPM, 2019[71]). This may inhibit investors' timely receipt of assistance and the Committee's ability to offer services that were not officially requested. Tajinvest is further constrained by its status as a State Unitary Enterprise with minimal legal power of its own (OECD interviews; Tajinvest, 2021).

When investors do manage to connect with the SCISPM, resolving issues for investors and pushing forward investment projects often requires co-ordination with other bodies (ministries, agencies, committees) through a whole-of-government approach. Despite reporting a high number of interactions with other institutions compared to other countries in the region, investors report that the SCISPM often been unable to resolve their issues with other agencies, especially the Tax Committee (OECD, 2020; OECD interviews, 2021). The SCISPM has no direct authority over many aspects of the investor experience, from registration to tax payment. Although the 2016 *Law on Investments* commits it to providing legal aid to investors, its charter does not include any mechanism for it to play the role of mediator between agencies in either a binding or advisory capacity (Government of the Republic of Tajikistan, 2006[55]).

Recommendation 3: Ease hurdles for investors and advocate on their behalf to encourage re-investments and improve the country's reputation

A strong public-private dialogue platform and individual advocacy when needed can help address investment climate issues

Effective policy advocacy is the most effective tool IPAs have to win investment, since much investment is re-investment from existing investors and positive investor experience begets a positive country reputation (OECD, 2011[72]). In the wake of the pandemic, which has rapidly changed economic conditions, OECD IPAs have devoted more time to dialogue with investors to comprehend administrative obstacles and establish priorities to ease operations. The usefulness of regulations can change; trade restrictions, public health limitations, inflation, and other changing market conditions may render incentives or regulations ineffective. It therefore makes sense to reassess regulatory regimes periodically for streamlining and simplification purposes through regular consultation with investors (and other stakeholders, such as domestic businesses). Often, existing investors share many concerns that affect decisions about new investments, so dialogue with a limited number of them has a strong chance to improve the business climate for all (OECD, 2015[23]).

Tajikistan's IPAs could improve regular and proactive collection of information from investors, which will feed into PPD. Mechanisms for dialogue with investors – prospective and current, large and small – can include regular meetings, feedback mechanisms for investors on the State Committee website, structured surveys, and periodic discussion forums on issues of interest to investors. Outcomes from these mechanisms could feed into the Consultative Council's regular meetings.

Dialogue, particularly if it is structured to cover general and industry-specific concerns of investors, requires time, staff, and funding. Given the need to make best use of limited resources, it could be useful to prioritise dialogues with investors in strategic sectors. Development partners and BIOs like the Chamber of Commerce and Industry could likely support Tajikistan's IPAs with facilitating dialogue or conducting surveys, since they already gather feedback from and have extensive contacts in the private sector. It is good practice to use various ways of collecting information from investors, like short surveys, because not all investors have time to dedicate to working group meetings or continuous dialogue. Yet, throughout conversations with investors it became clear that most investors in Tajikistan and elsewhere are content to dedicate time to improving the process (Box 10) (OECD, 2015[36]).

In many cases, structural reform will mitigate the need for individualised dispute resolution, but when conflicts arise, the SCISPM should be prepared to assist. To do this effectively, it needs to active and efficient co-operation of other ministries and state agencies involved in investment policy issues, like the Ministry of Economic Development and Trade and the Ministry of Justice. Fortunately, the SCISPM already has a strong relationship with other agencies through hosting joint events and other activities and enjoys high-level political support due to the government's strategic focus on investment promotion. However, it may nevertheless be useful to indicate what steps the SCISPM can take in the event that other institutions are unresponsive with respect to its concerns with respect to specific investor issues (OECD, 2011[72]). If this is done, the SCISPM will have the necessary clout and communication mechanisms to inform other agencies about investors' individual complaints and request that they be resolved before they escalate (UNCTAD, 2010[73]).

Box 9. Collecting investors' feedback through multiple channels: the case of the NFIA

The Dutch IPA, the Netherlands Foreign Investment Agency (NFIA), showcases how IPAs can collect feedback through multiple channels:

- Project managers in the IPA seeking daily feedback from a number of existing and potential investors;
- *Ad hoc* feedback through events or emails;
- Investor Relations' meetings;
- Triannual extended surveys among existing investors on the business climate;
- Quarterly meetings with the Invest in Holland Network directors;
- Analysis of lost projects by the NFIA; and
- Analysis of the media, external studies and reports on the Dutch business climate.

The feedback is then channelled to relevant decision-makers through:

- Annual reports to ministries (Ministry of Economic Affairs and Climate Policy and Ministry of Foreign Affairs) and discussions based thereon;
- Triannual reports on the results of the extended survey of the business climate; and
- Regular *ad hoc* discussions with the ministries.

Source: (de Combrugghe, 2019[74])

Tajikistan's IPAs can help investors by making information about regulations and administrative processes more available

Tajikistan may need to shift its resource distribution even more toward aftercare. In general, attracting new investors is more challenging and costly than supporting reinvestment and expansion (OECD, 2015[23]). COVID-19 further incentivised IPAs to shift their efforts and resources away from marketing and targeting and towards informing existing investors about government programmes, helping them cope with the crisis, and supporting their current investments and operations (OECD, 2020[15]). This has the effect of ensuring business continuity and investor satisfaction, which is critical for maintaining and expanding investments. OECD countries enhanced their facilitation activities and ensured service continuity through digital tools, such as virtual site visits. They strengthened dialogue with existing investors to monitor firm-level trends and respond quickly to potential problems, acting even more like "liaison officers" between governments and investors than usual.

Tajikistan's IPA should make it as easy as possible for investors to find information about rapidly changing economic conditions and pandemic-related policies. Most OECD IPAs created a dedicated COVID-19 section of the website with all relevant changes, including taxes, stimuli, export restrictions (OECD, 2020[15]). Some OECD IPAs, such as Spain and France, posted immediate English translations of new laws and regulations and prepared comprehensive sector-specific reports on the effects of COVID-19. Others, including Germany and Australia, offered daily updates. It is difficult to exaggerate the utility of providing reliable information in one dedicated spot, particularly where legislation is both complex and constantly evolving. This can take the form of updates in English and Russian on the B2B website.

Considering the relatively small number of foreign investors In Tajikistan, the SCISPM could even reach out to check in with investors and inform them about government measures affecting their investment. While it may be challenging at first to collect contact information without the benefit of a CRM system, this could serve as an impetus to create such a database, which will be valuable for years to come.

Box 10. IDA Ireland's outreach strategy about COVID-19 changes

Ireland has made information about COVID-19 very clear and easily available to investors:

- The front page of the website has a banner inviting investors to click for further information about IDA Ireland's COVID-19 updates and support. Investors can also navigate to this page from anywhere on the website by clicking "How we help" in the header.
- The first link on the COVID-19 page invites investors to contact their account manager or the general IDA Ireland e-mail for free advice on accessing government support and funding, while also providing a button to access more information about these programmes. A government-run hotline for businesses is also available.
- A brief yet highly useful response plan reassures investors that the IPA's goal is to help them weather the crisis. The plan includes specific information about consulting services available and the application process for IPA funding. Many relevant links are also provided, like the government's list of essential services, payroll and tax support information, and loans for SMEs.
- Relevant publications from other government agencies are, such as Enterprise Ireland's guide to HR in the post-pandemic environment and health and travel advice, are consolidated on the website.
- Monthly e-magazines and e-mailed newsletters are freely available and include even more detailed updates than regular news articles.

IDA Ireland also prioritised collecting information *from* investors about their new challenges through a client assessment process of firm responses and supply chain disruptions.

Source: (IDA Ireland, 2021[75])

Both during the pandemic and beyond, investors would benefit from clearer information on the services and requirements – digital and not – that are offered by other government agencies. Digital services, such as the tax payment portal and the e-visa, should be clearly linked on the IPA's website with detailed instructions. This would also help resolve language issues because investors would not need to navigate non-English websites of other agencies. For paper-based services, the IPAs should provide PDF versions of forms that need to be submitted and comprehensive information on how to submit them, including the contact information of the relevant agency. Furthermore, the process of requesting assistance from the SCISPM in fulfilling other agencies' bureaucratic requirements should be dramatically simplified. Instead of having to upload relevant documents – including those that investors may need help obtaining, such as proof of registration – a basic request should be enough at least to obtain a meeting. At that point, the SCISPM can request only the documents necessary to fulfil the other agency's requirement. In this way, the SCISPM will be a helpful facilitator rather than an *additional* bureaucratic hassle.

On top of obtaining reliable information, investors rely on IPAs to continue their operations. Particularly amidst COVID-19 and interrupted supply chains – which could even affect crucial health and food imports – investors need reliable networks with domestic firms. Some OECD agencies, including Czech Invest, Enterprise Greece and the Polish Investment and Trade Agency stepped up their existing matchmaking services by making use of virtual platforms (OECD, 2020[15]). Tajikistan's B2B portal has contact information for some companies, mostly in Russian. Ensuring this is all translated into English and potentially improving or individualising this matchmaking mechanism would be useful to investors in such uncertain times. Georgia also provides a good example in creating guidebooks for investors, which are regularly updated on the website (Box 12).

Box 11. Invest in Georgia's partnership with global advisory companies and its role as an information provider

Representative offices abroad are some of the most effective mechanisms for FDI attraction. However, smaller countries cannot always afford operating such offices in various places. In order to tackle this challenge, Georgia has undertaken the following measures:

- Development of special Investment attraction guidebooks for Georgia's Diplomats abroad. The guidebook includes, consolidated information on sectors that are prioritized in terms of FDI attraction, as well as "Talking points" with potential companies. With this, Invest in Georgia conducted special training sessions with the embassies to make them more acquainted with the investment proposition of the country.
- With the support of USAID Georgia and USAID Invest, Invest in Georgia contracted a global advisory company - OCO Global, which partially fulfils the duties of offices abroad for Invest in Georgia. More precisely, the company is responsible to contact potential investors on behalf of Invest in Georgia in various countries and facilitates meetings with companies that have interest to invest in Georgia. The contract is developed with specific KPIs, including number of meetings to be conducted, site visits to be organized and potential deals to be concluded. This experience has allowed Georgia to contact hundreds of companies through facilitators in foreign countries, without actually having to establish and operate representative offices abroad.

In addition, Invest in Georgia has developed a number of investment guidebooks in partnership with internationally well-known companies like the "Big 4". These cover a variety of legislative issues and explain to investors the labour laws, customs procedures, issues related to privatization, company registration, obtaining various permits and licenses, and other relevant topics. Overall, 11 roadmaps containing information have been developed and are updated on annual basis. With this, Georgia only runs and promotes a single web page – investingeorgia.org.

Source: Enterprise Georgia.

In the long term, it may be desirable to grant more authority to the SCISPM such that they could provide required services directly through the single-window mechanism. This would significantly simplify the investment process and make Tajikistan more competitive for investors, since most Eurasia IPAs have a one-stop-shop already (OECD, 2020[27]).

Simplifying investment project approval processes and using the investment agreement as a tool to pre-emptively protect investors from legal disputes are under the SCISPM's control

Since the process of approving an investment is one over which the SCISPM has full control, unlike many other investor services areas like registration and customs, it is highly recommended that the Committee digitise the investment approval process. The first step is providing detailed information about criteria and requirements on the website (which should be minimised and simplified), and the second step is introducing an online application. This will increase transparency and reduce bureaucratic hurdles for investors. In cases of rejection, the SCISPM should publish the reasons and allow appeal. Enhancing trust at this early stage of investment will encourage investors to stay in Tajikistan, re-invest, and share their positive experience with potential investors.

According to its charter, the SCISPM also has statutory authority to negotiate and sign investment agreements on behalf of the government. Ultimately, though, the *Law on Investment Agreements* stipulates that they be approved and ratified by the government and parliament (Government of the Republic of Tajikistan, 2006[55]; 2017[76]). This can create several potential bottlenecks. Another concern is that the government can offer the project to another investor through an open tender, in which the winning investor compensates the one who proposed the project for expenses incurred but not the intellectual property involved (U.S. Department of State, 2020[70]; Government of Tajikistan, 2013[77]). Therefore, it would be desirable to remove the possibility of an open tender when an investor proposes a project – essentially only allowing the government to accept or refuse the investment.

Nevertheless, according to interviews with investors and government stakeholders, the investor agreement has proven as a reliable tool in the past that creates a safety net for investors, rendering it nearly impossible to change regulations. Therefore, in line with the SCISPM's charter, the government should empower the Committee to encourage investors to sign an agreement, negotiate with them, and sign it with as few other approvals as possible. The *Law on Investment Agreements* provides for several benefits that can be included in agreements:

- Special incentives and advantages in areas like taxes, customs, permission to act in violation of anti-monopoly laws, and regulatory requirements (e.g., licensing);
- A commitment that any future legislation worsening the investment climate would not apply to the investment project; and
- A provision that disputes will be resolved in an international arbitration forum rather than Tajikistan's courts (which is otherwise the default mechanism, as per the *Law on Investment Agreements*).

The last point is especially an important protection for investors given the legal issues that investors encounter in Tajikistan, although unfortunately as of now Tajikistan does not always enforce international arbitration awards (OECD, 2021[2]).

Way forward

This section presents a timeline for implementing the policy recommendations given throughout the report. It takes into account the need for the government to 1) make sure the proper tools for promotional activities are in place 2) strengthen the institutional setting and strategy of investment promotion, and 3) ensure a well-functioning facilitation system and better leverage the policy advocacy function. Further work on the recommendations will follow in OECD capacity-building workshops that will support implementation in 2022 and 2023. The workshops will be led by the State Committee for Investment and State Property Management and will include other stakeholders that can support the implementation process. The OECD will assist the process and invite experts to share their knowledge on the relevant policy areas.

To conclude, the OECD would like to emphasise the importance of the cross-cutting recommendations noted in the introduction.

I. Co-ordination, consolidation, and a whole-of-government approach go beyond just IPAs. Aligning priorities and creating productive communication channels with other government agencies, such as the Tax Committee and the administrations of the FEZs, would significantly improve the investor experience when legal disputes arise, since the IPA could serve as an official mediator. Even simply ensuring that IPA websites have clear links to other agencies' relevant services and that technical information is consistent across sites would be a large improvement in giving investors a less confusing, whole-of-government experience.

II. Ensuring sufficient staff with the skills to attract and retain investors remains a priority across the board. The SCISPM has many mandates yet few staff members. The lack of employees with private sector experience means that they do not necessarily have the full spectrum of needed skills to engage with investors, such as expertise in marketing. Of course, increasing the budget and financial autonomy of the IPAs would allow them to hire more staff members with strong skills, yet with COVID-19 affecting the budget moving forward, other methods will have to accommodate. IPAs will need to "work smarter, not harder" in order to compensate for the small number of employees in Tajikistan's resource-constrained environment. Clear prioritisation of tasks through an overarching investment strategy and specific sectoral targeting will maximise the impact of each staff member by ensuring they are spending their time on the most productive activities. Time-consuming investment promotion activities, like frequent events and news articles for websites, may not be as important as simple solutions like keeping track of investor information in a database. Digitalisation can help maximise the impact of a small staff as well. The more information that is easily accessible on a website and the more services that are digitised, the less work there will be for staff members responding to inquiries and providing routine services. This will allow them to spend their time on tasks that have a higher value-added for investors and therefore are more likely to lead to further investment, like customised targeting and support with legal issues.

III. The third theme is participating in the international investment promotion community to support the implementation of these recommendations and ensure continued adoption of best practices in the future as external circumstances evolve. Exchanges among peers on lessons-learned is both critical for short-term adaptation, as has become especially clear during the COVID-19 crisis, and as well as long-term strategic planning, particularly in the post-pandemic world (OECD, 2020[15]). Throughout this report and in related working group and capacity-building events, the OECD has drawn on lessons from IPAs around the world and invited international experts to share their experiences. It will continue to do so in the implementation-support activities that will be undertaken in 2022. However, this is just the start. The OECD founded its IPA Network, comprised of senior IPA officials of OECD and partner countries, in 2016 to encourage dialogue and the exchange of experience (OECD, 2020[15]). The OECD IPA network shares its expertise with peers from other parts of the world and will continue to be a resource on which Tajikistan can draw in the future.

Recommendation	Short term (6 months-1 year)	Medium term (1-2 years)	Long term (3-5 years)
Recommendation 1: Make sure the proper tools for promotional activities are in place	• Develop a clear and realistic value proposition and put it on websites • Analyse pre-existing work and studies on viable target sectors to create a long-list of potential priority sectors • Prioritise updating websites for simplicity, consistency, English translations, and working links • Create a CRM system or at least a shared database and begin to store investor information there	• Conduct a more detailed analysis of Tajikistan's comparative advantages in each sector for sector-specific value propositions • Select 3-5 specific priority sectors along with target countries and projects. Include these in the overall investment promotion strategy (above), and revise *all* government websites and publications accordingly • Create mechanisms to collect potential investors' contacts from website and analyse site visits • Research potential investors, especially through a collaborative regional approach, and include them in the CRM system • Proactively reach out to targeted investors	• Consolidate all IPA websites into just one • Assign staff members to specific potential investors to develop lasting relationships
Recommendation 2: Strengthen the institutional setting and strategy of investment promotion	• Make a detailed plan for the development of an investment promotion strategy, including timeline, resources, and research methods with public and private stakeholders	• Clarify the roles and mandates of institutions active in investment promotion through the harmonisation of laws and IPAs' charters • Develop and approve a whole-of-government investment promotion strategy, including overall goals, SWOT analysis, M&E mechanisms, and specific methods for investment promotion that maximise institutional collaboration rather than duplication • Create recruitment mechanisms to attract employees from the private sector	• Allocate sufficient and up to 3-year funding for IPAs in state budget to ensure financial stability and independence • Align IPA mandates with resources
Recommendation 3: Better leverage the policy advocacy function and improve the facilitation system	• Include a COVID-19 section on the IPA websites with policy and economic changes and consider newsletters or individual outreach to current investors to assess current challenges and offer support • Collaborate with BIOs and the development community to maximise information collection on the effects of the pandemic and use this information in policy advocacy • Simplify or remove the application process for requesting assistance from the SCISPM • Showcase the investment agreement as a tool on the IPA websites	• Re-allocate resources toward facilitation and aftercare • Add links on the IPA websites to all relevant government agencies' services and requirements and create detailed instructions for obtaining and fulfilling these • Simplify and digitalise the investment approval process • Increase the frequency and diversity of dialogue opportunities with investors, such as surveys, to collect information on challenges with the investment framework • Expand matchmaking services on the B2B portal • Improve legal support for investors by establishing formal communication channels with top decision-makers	• Empower the SCISPM's single-window to provide investor services directly • Revise the Law on Investment Agreements to allow the SCISPM greater freedom to negotiate and conclude investment agreements on behalf of the state

Annex A. Data Collection

Interviews

To better understand the situation in Tajikistan and replace the missions that the OECD usually conducts, the OECD team held a series of interviews (approximately 25) over a period of six months. The interviewees ranged from investors to government authorities, international organisations, embassies, business associations, researchers, and more. Interviewees will not be disclosed. The questions aimed at receiving an impression of the current business and investment climate, including relevant challenges. Carried out over zoom, the interviews provided snapshots of individual perceptions; in aggregate, the interviews support crucial arguments given throughout the paper.

In general, it is important to note that surveys or interviews may not be regarded as unbiased information. Sources of bias may include the relationship of the interviewer and the interviewee, the social standing of the participants, or the wording of the questions (Holstein & Gubrium, 1997).

Virtual working Groups

Within the framework of the OECD Eurasia Competitiveness Programme (ECP), the OECD and the government of Tajikistan established a public-private working group to develop guidelines and recommendations for enhancing investment promotion practises in Tajikistan. The Working Group brought together representatives from government agencies, investors, business associations such as the Chamber of Commerce and Industry, and other development partners. The OECD ECP, with contributions from international experts and peer reviewers from OECD member countries, carried out analysis, data collection and consultations with stakeholders in Tajikistan to identify the main issues and the most effective policy responses to improve Tajikistan's investment promotion practices.

Several virtual working groups meetings took place in preparation for the peer review of Tajikistan:

- **28 January 2021:** first meeting of the Working Group to frame issues and share insights with local stakeholders;
- **17 June 2021:** second meeting of the Working Group with international experts to discuss preliminary recommendations;
- **5 October 2021:** third meeting of the Working Group with international experts to discuss the peer review note and its recommendations.

This report was peer reviewed on date at the eight session of the OECD Eurasia Competitiveness Roundtable, a policy network that brings together high-level representatives and technical experts from Eurasia countries, OECD members and partner organisations. The Roundtable meets annually and serves as a platform for peer review and knowledge sharing on the implementation of competitiveness reforms in the Eurasia region.

The peer review aimed to help Tajikistan define further steps for policy reform implementation. In particular, the roundtable discussion was facilitated by the following experts, who provided an overview of the current situation in Tajikistan and insights into the experiences of OECD and Eurasia countries:

- Ms Diana Ablyakimova, Director, Kazakh Invest

- Mr Tornike Zirakishvili, Deputy Director, Enterprise Georgia
- Mr Philippe Yvergniaux, Expert, Business France

In addition, OECD experts from the Secretariat – who had previously provided their insights and reviews to the peer review note – participated in the discussions.

Progress towards implementing these recommendations could be discussed in two years' time at the 2023 OECD Eurasia Competitiveness Roundtable.

Questionnaires

The OECD also relied on information from the OECD IPA survey that has been conducted for OECD countries and different regions. These surveys, based on a comprehensive survey jointly designed with the Inter-American Development Bank, provide comparative evidence across agencies, categorise their profiles, and explain existing trends and practices in investment promotion and facilitation. Tajikistan (Tajinvest and SCISPM) had filled the survey in 2019, as part of their review for the *Mapping of Investment Promotion Agencies in Eurasia*.

To receive updated and additional information, the OECD:

- sent an updated and tailored version of the IPA questionnaire to the SCISPM
- sent a shortened version of the IPA questionnaire to other government stakeholders.

References

ADB (2021), *Per Capita GDP Growth in Asia and the Pacific, Asian Development Outlook (ADO)*, https://data.adb.org/dataset/capita-gdp-growth-asia-and-pacific-asian-development-outlook. [12]

Agency for the Promotion and Protection of Investments of the Kyrgyz Republic (2021), *Success Stories*, https://invest.gov.kg/. [34]

Agency on Statistics under the President of Tajikistan (2020), *Macroeconomic Indicators*, https://www.stat.tj/en/macroeconomic-indicators. [6]

Avesta (2018), *Алюминиевый спад: В Таджикистане последние 6 лет идет спад производства алюминия*, http://avesta.tj/2018/01/22/alyuminievyj-spad-v-tadzhikistane-poslednie-6-let-idet-spad-proizvodstva-alyuminiya/. [92]

BCG (2018), *Investing in Central Asia*, https://image-src.bcg.com/Images/BCG-Investing-In-Central-Asia-report-ENG_tcm9-247778.pdf. [91]

Blavatnik School of Government (2020), *Oxford COVID-19 Government Response Tracker*, https://github.com/OxCGRT/covid-policy-scratchpad/tree/master/regional_reports/archived_regional_reports. [60]

Byrne, P. (2016), *Major Structural Components of an Investment Promotion Strategy*, Background paper to an OECD workshop on investment promotion in Bishkek. [47]

Caribbean Export Development Agency (2014), *The Development and Implementation of National Investment Promotion Strategies*, https://www.ceintelligence.com/files/documents/NIPS_Handbook.pdf. [53]

Carole Biau (2015), *Regional Investment: Time to Cooperate*, http://oecdinsights.org/2015/07/16/regional-investment-time-to-cooperate/. [41]

Center for Regional Economic Competitiveness (2021), *Step 2: Developing Effective Value Propositions*, https://www.usacompetes.com/plan-strategize/developing-an-fdi-strategy-and-plan/how-do-i-define-the-value-proposition-that-will-best-differentiate-our-area-and-effectively-attract-foreign-investors/. [40]

Clarity Business Strategies (2018), *Developing Outstanding Inward Investment Value Propositions: 5 Key Principles for Success*, https://www.clarity-strategies.com/2016/04/inward-investment-value-proposition.html. [43]

Consultative Council on Improvement of Investment Climate under the President of the Republic of Tajikistan (2021), *Main Achievements*, http://investmentcouncil.tj/en/council/monitoring/achievements/. [62]

Consultative Council on Improvement of Investment Climate under the President of the Republic of Tajikistan (2020), *Results of Decision Implementation of 20th Session*, http://investmentcouncil.tj/upload/iblock/8d8/3_Monitoring%20Matrix.pdf. [63]

Customs Service (2021), *Single Window Centre*, https://www.swcustoms.tj/. [65]

de Combrugghe, A. (2019), *Supporting Investment Climate Reforms through Policy Advocacy*, https://www.oecd.org/investment/investment-policy/Investment-Insights-Supporting-investment-climate-reforms-through-IPA-policy-advocacy.pdf (accessed on 2 August 2021). [74]

EBRD (2020), *Tajikistan Diagnostic*, https://www.ebrd.com/where-we-are/tajikistan/overview.html. [18]

Embassy of Switzerland in Tajikistan (2020), "Annual Economic Report 2020", *Tajikistan*, https://www.s-ge.com/sites/default/files/publication/free/economic-report-tajikistan-eda-2020-07.pdf (accessed on 14 May 2021). [93]

Embassy of Switzerland in Tajikistan (2020), "Tajikistan", *Annual Economic Report 2020*, https://www.s-ge.com/sites/default/files/publication/free/economic-report-tajikistan-eda-2020-07.pdf. [19]

Eurasianet (2018), *Tajikistan Adopts Partial Moratorium on Business Inspections*, https://eurasianet.org/tajikistan-adopts-partial-moratorium-on-business-inspections. [69]

FEZ "Dangara" (2018), *FEZ "Dangara"*, http://fezdangara.tj/. [32]

FEZ "Panch" & OSCE (2009), *Free Economic Zone "Panch"*, http://fezpanj.tj/ru/home.html. [33]

Government of Tajikistan (2016), *Закон об инвестициях [Law on Investments] No. 196.* [59]

Government of Tajikistan (2013), *LAW OF RT «ON INVESTMENT AGREEMENT»*, http://tpp.tj/business-guide2017/pdf/pdf_eng/02%20-%20Law%20of%20the%20Republic%20of%20Tajikistan%20On%20investment%20agreement.pdf (accessed on 21 December 2021). [77]

Government of Tajikistan (2012), *Концепция государственной политики привлечения и защиты инвестиций Республики Таджикистан [Concept of State Policy for the Attraction and Protection of Investments of the Republic of Tajikistan] No. 755.* [25]

Government of the Republic of Tajikistan (2017), *Закон Республики Таджикистан об ивестиционном соглашении [Law of the Republic of Tajikistan about investment agreements] No. 1435.* [76]

Government of the Republic of Tajikistan (2006), *Положение о Государственном комитете по инвестициям и управлению государственным имуществом Республики Таджикистан [Provision on the State Committee for Investments and State Property Management of the Republic of Tajikistan] No. 590.* [55]

Harding, T. and B. Javorcik (2012), *Investment Promotion and FDI Inflows: Quality Matters*, University of Oxford Economic Series Working Papers 612, https://users.ox.ac.uk/~econ0247/MIGA.pdf. [44]

Healy Consultants (2021), *Fees and Timelines*, https://www.healyconsultants.com/tajikistan-company-registration/fees-timelines/#timelines. [86]

IBT Partners (2020), *Optimizing Your Online Presence: Digital Strategies for Investment Promotion Agencies*, https://cdn2.hubspot.net/hub/209596/file-311416263-pdf/docs/French_Gov_-_Optimising_your_Online_Presence.pdf. [50]

IDA Ireland (2021), *COVID-19 Updates & Support*, https://www.idaireland.com/how-we-help/covid19-support-and-updates. [75]

IDA Ireland (2021), *Driving Recovery and Sustainable Growth*, https://www.idaireland.com/getmedia/4caa3e4c-f68c-40f3-bc40-5902034514ff/IDA_STRATEGY_Draft_15.pdf.aspx. [58]

IMF (2021), *World Economic Outlook*, https://www.imf.org/en/Publications/WEO/weo-database/2021/April. [7]

InvestChile (2021), *Why Invest in Chile*, https://investchile.gob.cl/why-chile/. [78]

Investment Promotion Center of CCPIT (2021), *Platform Service*, http://en.investchinaccpit.com/p112/ptfw.html. [68]

Kaymaz, N. (2019), *Investment Promotion and Lead Generation: Turkey's Experience*, Presentation at the 4th Meeting of the OECD Investment Promotion Agency (IPA) Network by the Presidency of the Republic of Turkey Investment Office. [49]

Kazakh Invest (2021), *About Kazakh Invest*, https://invest.gov.kz/about-us/kazakh-invest/. [56]

Kazakh Invest (2021), *Success Story*, https://invest.gov.kz/about-kazakhstan/success-story/. [35]

Kemp, S. (2021), *Digital 2021: Tajikistan*, https://datareportal.com/reports/digital-2021-tajikistan. [79]

Kosymova, Z. and N. Abdujabborov (2015), *From Regional to National PPD in Tajikistan*, CIPE, http://ppd.cipe.org/wp-content/uploads/2016/03/2015-Public-Private-Dialogue-in-Tajikistan.pdf. [61]

Loewendahl, H. and S. Bryan (2019), *Guidelines for Developing an Investment Promotion Strategy*, Canada-Indonesia Trade and Private Sector Assistance Project, http://www.tpsaproject.com/wp-content/uploads/2019-02-28-Manual-1124.08c.pdf. [52]

Millenium Cities Initiative (2009), *Handbook for Promoting Foreign Direct Investment in Medium-Sized, Low-Budget Cities in Emerging Markets*, Vale Columbia Center on Sustainable International Investment, http://mci.ei.columbia.edu/files/2012/12/MCI-City-Investment-Promotion-Handbook2.pdf. [57]

Ministry of Foreign Affairs (2021), *E-Visa Tajikistan*, https://www.evisa.tj/index.evisa.html. [64]

Mirsaidov, N. (2021), *Таджикистан внедряет реформы, чтобы привлечь зарубежные инвестиции [Tajikistan is implementing reforms to attract foreign investment]*, Karavansarai, https://central.asia-news.com/ru/articles/cnmi_ca/features/2021/03/11/feature-01. [28]

Moody's (2020), *Rating Action: Moody's affirms Tajikistan's B3 rating; outlook remains negative*, https://www.moodys.com/research/Moodys-affirms-Tajikistans-B3-rating-outlook-remains-negative--PR_418888. [94]

Moody's (2020), *Rating Action: Moody's Affirms Tajikistan's B3 Rating; Outlook Remains Negative*, https://www.moodys.com/research/Moodys-affirms-Tajikistans-B3-rating-outlook-remains-negative--PR_418888. [87]

National Bank of Tajikistan (2020), *Платежный баланс, международная инвестиционная позиция Республики Таджикистан [Balance of Payments, International Investment Position of the Republic of Tajikistan]*, https://www.nbt.tj/ru/statistics/tavozuni-pardokhti-jt/tavozuni-pardokhti-jumhurii-tojikiston/nashriyai_tavozuni_pardoht_mavkei.php. [89]

Nurgozhayeva, R. (2020), *How China's Belt and Road is Changing Central Asia*, The Diplomat, https://thediplomat.com/2020/07/how-is-chinas-belt-and-road-changing-central-asia/#:~:text=For%20Central%20Asia%2C%20BRI%20projects,modernize%20their%20obsolete%20transport%20infrastructure.&text=Although%20the%20BRI%20is%20an,criticism%2C%20especially%20. [83]

Observatory of Economic Complexity (2019), *Tajikistan*, https://oec.world/en/profile/country/tjk. [90]

OECD (2021), *Crude oil import prices*, https://data.oecd.org/energy/crude-oil-import-prices.htm. [9]

OECD (2021), *Improving the Legal Environment for Business and Investment in Central Asia*, https://www.oecd.org/eurasia/Improving-LEB-CA-ENG%2020%20April.pdf. [2]

OECD (2021), *Informality and Covid-19 in Eurasia: The Sudden Loss of a Social Buffer*, https://www.oecd.org/eurasia/COVID-19-informality-Eurasia.pdf. [84]

OECD (2020), *COVID-19 Crisis Response in Central Asia*, https://www.oecd.org/coronavirus/policy-responses/covid-19-crisis-response-in-central-asia-5305f172/#:~:text=linklink%20copied!-,Context,OECD%2C%202020%5B19%5D). [10]

OECD (2020), *Investment Promotion Agencies in the Time of Covid-19*, https://www.oecd.org/coronavirus/policy-responses/investment-promotion-agencies-in-the-time-of-covid-19-50f79678/. [15]

OECD (2020), *Investment Promotion in Eurasia: A Mapping of Investment Promotion Agencies*, https://www.oecd.org/eurasia/competitiveness-programme/Investment-Promotion-in-Eurasia-A-Mapping-of-Investment-Promotion-Agencies-ENG.pdf. [27]

OECD (2020), *OECD Investment Policy Reviews: Egypt 2020*, https://www.oecd-ilibrary.org/sites/98f6a4b7-en/index.html?itemId=/content/component/98f6a4b7-en. [51]

OECD (2019), *Mapping of Investment Promotion Agencies Middle East and North Africa*, https://www.oecd.org/investment/Mapping-of-Investment-Promotion-Agencies-MED.pdf. [22]

OECD (2018), *Mapping of Investment Promotion Agencies in OECD Countries*, https://www.oecd.org/investment/Mapping-of-Investment-Promotion-Agencies-in-OECD-Countries.htm. [20]

OECD (2015), *Policy Framework for Investment*, https://www.oecd.org/investment/pfi.htm. [23]

OECD (2015), *Strengthening Chile's Investment Promotion Strategy*, https://www.oecd.org/daf/inv/investment-policy/Chile-investment-promotion-strategy-2015.pdf. [36]

OECD (2011), *Policy Framework for Investment: User's Toolkit*, https://www.oecd.org/investment/toolkit/policyareas/investmentpromotionfacilitation/41246119.pdf. [72]

OECD (2010), *Competitiveness and Private Sector Development: Kazakhstan Sector Competitiveness Strategy*, https://www.oecd-ilibrary.org/finance-and-investment/competitiveness-and-private-sector-development-kazakhstan-2010_9789264089792-en. [45]

OECD (Forthcoming), *COVID-19 in Central Asia: Mitigation, Recovery and Reform.* [85]

OECD & Inter-American Development Bank (2019), *How to Solve the Investment Promotion Puzzle: A Mapping of Investment Promotion Agencies in Latin America and the Caribbean and OECD Countries*, https://publications.iadb.org/en/how-solve-investment-promotion-puzzle-mapping-investment-promotion-agencies-latin-america-and. [21]

Santander Trade (2021), *Tajikistan: Foreign Investment*, https://santandertrade.com/en/portal/establish-overseas/tajikistan/investing-3?url_de_la_page=%2Fen%2Fportal%2Festablish-overseas%2Ftajikistan%2Finvesting-3&&actualiser_id_banque=oui&id_banque=0&memoriser_choix=memoriser. [17]

Schwab, K. (2019), *The Global Economic Competitiveness Report*, World Economic Forum, http://www3.weforum.org/docs/WEF_TheGlobalCompetitivenessReport2019.pdf. [24]

SCISPM (2019), *Required Documents*, https://investcom.tj/en/investments/single-window/183-required-documents.html. [71]

SCISPM (2018), *Service List*, https://investcom.tj/en/investments/single-window/182-service-list.html. [80]

SCISPM & TajInvest (2020), *Tajikistan launches a Single Window system for registering export-import transactions*, https://b2b.tj/en/news/details/a4d39508-2240-42d6-9d00-33acc2814308#:~:text=According%20to%20the%20country's%20customs,export%2Dimport%20and%20transit%20operations. [66]

SCISPM & TajInvest (2018), *First Steps to Startup [sic] Business in Tajikistan*, https://b2b.tj/en/news/details/dabb1859-9aba-472c-91f3-09bb0190a07d. [81]

SCISPM, TajInvest, GIZ, & OSCE (2019), *Business Portal*, https://b2b.tj/ru/home/default. [29]

SPISPM (2018), *Государственный комитет по инвестициям и управлению государственным имуществом Республики Таджикистан [State Committee for Investments and State Property Management]*, https://investcom.tj/langru.html (accessed on 2 July 2021). [30]

SugdNEWS (2020), *"Спитамен Текстайл" привлекает южнокорейские инвестиции и технологии ["Spitamen Textile" attracts South Korean investments and technolgies]*, http://sugdnews.com/2020/03/17/spitamen-tekstajl-privlekaet-juzhnokorejskie-investicii-i-tehnologii-2/. [48]

TajInvest (2021), *Obtaining a Visa*, http://tajinvest.tj/en/investors/pribytie-v-tadzhikistan. [82]

TajInvest (2021), *Устав предприятия [Charter of the enterprise]*, https://tajinvest.tj/ru/about-us/ustav. [88]

TajInvest (2019), *TajInvest*, http://tajinvest.tj/ru/ (accessed on 2 July 2021). [31]

Tax Committee (2021), *Все электронные сервисы [All electronic services]*, https://andoz.tj/Services?culture=ru-RU. [67]

Tsimal, S. (2020), *Is investment promotion a digital or a people business?*, https://www.citynationplace.com/investment-promotion-digital-or-human-sirpa-tsimal. [54]

U.S. Department of State (2020), *2020 Investment Climate Statements: Tajikistan*, https://www.state.gov/reports/2020-investment-climate-statements/tajikistan/. [70]

UN ESCAP (2019), *Investment Promotion and Image Building Strategy and Tools*, National Workshop on Promotion and Facilitation of Foreign Direct Investment for Sustainable Development in Timur Leste, United Nations Economic and Social Commission for Asia and the Pacific, https://www.unescap.org/sites/default/files/Session%204-Image%20building%20and%20investment%20promotion.pdf. [42]

UNCTAD (2021), "Investment Trends Monitor", *Special WIF Factsheet Edition*, https://unctad.org/system/files/official-document/diaeiainf2021d2_en.pdf (accessed on 20 December 2021). [14]

UNCTAD (2020), *Foreign Direct Investment: Inward and outward flow and stock, annual*, https://unctadstat.unctad.org/wds/TableViewer/tableView.aspx?ReportId=96740. [13]

UNCTAD (2020), *Foreign Direct Investment: Inward and outward flow and stock, annual*, https://unctadstat.unctad.org/wds/TableViewer/tableView.aspx?ReportId=96740. [95]

UNCTAD (2016), *Investment Policy Review: Kyrgyzstan*, https://inff.org/assets/resource/kyrgyzstan---investment-policy-review.pdf. [46]

UNCTAD (2016), *Investment Policy Review: Tajikistan*, https://unctad.org/system/files/official-document/diaepcb2016d1_en.pdf. [26]

UNCTAD (2010), *Investor-State Disputes: Prevention and Alternatives to Arbitration*, https://unctad.org/system/files/official-document/diaeia200911_en.pdf. [73]

Wadhwa, K. and S. Reddy (2011), "Foreign Direct Investment into Developing Asian Countries: The Role of Market Seeking, Resource Seeking and Efficiency Seeking Factors", *International Journal of Business and Management*, Vol. 6/11. [39]

WAIPA (2020), *IPA Toolbox: A Practical Guide to Support Investment Promotion Agencies*, Deutsche Gesellschaft für Internationale Zusammenarbeit (GIZ), https://waipa.org/waipa-content/uploads/IPA-Toolbox-2020.pdf. [37]

World Bank (2021), *Foreign direct investment, net inflows (% of GDP)*, https://data.worldbank.org/indicator/BX.KLT.DINV.WD.GD.ZS. [16]

World Bank (2021), *Personal remittances, received (current US$) - Tajikistan*, https://data.worldbank.org/indicator/BX.TRF.PWKR.CD.DT?locations=TJ. [8]

World Bank (2021), *Tajikistan Economic Update summer 2021*, https://www.worldbank.org/en/country/tajikistan/publication/economic-update-summer-2021. [1]

World Bank (2021), *The World Bank in Tajikistan*, https://www.worldbank.org/en/country/tajikistan/overview. [4]

World Bank (2020), *Rebuilding Investor Confidence in Times of Uncertainty*, https://openknowledge.worldbank.org/handle/10986/33808. [38]

World Bank (2020), *Tajikistan Economic Update – Fall 2020*, https://www.worldbank.org/en/country/tajikistan/publication/economic-update-fall-2020. [11]

World Bank (2019), *GDP growth (annual %)*, https://data.worldbank.org/indicator/NY.GDP.MKTP.KD.ZG?locations=TJ. [5]

World Bank (2019), *Poverty headcount ratio at national poverty lines (% of population) - Tajikistan*, https://data.worldbank.org/indicator/SI.POV.NAHC?locations=TJ. [3]

Notes

[1] *"Project funded by the European Commission and carried out by Luvent Consulting (Safege consortium)"*

[2] Inflows to Azerbaijan, Kazakhstan and Turkmenistan over the period averaged 15.1, 7.5 and 7.6%, respectively.

[3] According to the World Bank, foreign direct investment collapsed by 47% year-over-year in 2020.

[4] Assistance with project definition, information on local suppliers/ clients, working meetings, site visits; assistance with administrative procedures, such as business/ tax registrations, obtaining licenses/ land and construction approvals, visas and work permits, with utilities; legal issues; assistance in obtaining financing; aftercare services: structured trouble shooting; mitigation of conflicts; matchmaking, linkages and other business support programmes (database of local suppliers; capacity-building support for local firms; matchmaking service between investors and local firms)

[5] poultry farming, fish farming, the securities market, free economic zones, innovative and technological activities; construction of hydroelectric power plants, newly created and operating enterprises that include the full range of processing cotton fibre into final products

[6] In particular, amendments were made to the Law of the Republic of Tajikistan "On Enforcement Proceedings" dated January 2, 2019 year, no. 1562 and to the first and second parts of the Civil Code of 01/02/2019, No. 1557 and No. 1558.

www.ingramcontent.com/pod-product-compliance
Lightning Source LLC
Chambersburg PA
CBHW061225240926
51846CB00006B/1358